To El

Enjoy!

MW01146449

SCOREKEEPER FOR THE MET

SCOREKEEPER FOR THE MET

*Stories of the
Chief Music Librarian
of the Metropolitan Opera*

JOHN
GRANDE

*Full Court Press
Englewood Cliffs, New Jersey*

First Edition

Copyright © 2015 by John Grande

Published in the United States of America by Full Court Press, 601 Palisade Avenue Englewood Cliffs, NJ 07632 fullcourtpressnj.com

ISBN 978-1-938812-66-8 Library of Congress Control No. 2015951610

Editing and Book Design by Barry Sheinkopf for Bookshapers (bookshapers.com)

Colophon by Liz Sedlack

ACKNOWLEDGMENTS

My heart and thoughts are filled with gratitude for the many wonderful people who have deeply touched my life. At this moment I am pressed to mention a few of them, though there are certainly many others worthy of mention. You will read about those people, who helped me along the way.

First and foremost I must express my gratitude to my loving and supportive parents, Frank and Mary, who encouraged me to follow my dreams. My father, my sister Mary, and one of my brothers, Joe, were excellent musicians, so it followed that I too would explore the musical world.

My beloved wife, Joan, has always been there for me the last fifty-plus years. Her beautiful voice, which is remarkable even today, continues to be a source of great joy and pride for me. She could easily have flown to operatic heights, except that being a mother and wife were her priority, so her rising career, and her opportunities to shine, were cut short—though she accepted many of them over the years when they did not interfere with our family life. For this, and for my two wonderful sons, Mickey and John, I will be eternally grateful.

Harry Schumer, my mentor, who was the Chief Librarian when I first began working for the Met Opera, was a great help in getting my career launched. I had very little experience in the beginning, but thanks to his instructions, I was asked, on his retirement, to be his replacement. I was in the right place at the right time, and supported by the right people. "God's hand!"

Now that I have retired, I have the luxury of writing, among other endeavors. Fortunately, I have joined a creative writing group that has given me the impetus to hone my skills, and I believe that what I have shared with them should be shared with a wider audience. Thanks to the group's leader, Elizabeth Larson, I am now ready to proceed with the venture. *Enjoy!*

Since many of these stories were written years ago, at times some redundancies may have crept in. Also, I at times use the word "Met" instead of "Metropolitan Opera." I trust the reader will forgive the license.

TABLE OF CONTENTS

My Life

And So…I Was Born, *3*

A Pain In The Butt, *5*

Grammar School, *7*

Pop, *9*

The Shot Heard Round The World—And In Astoria, *11*

Double Trouble, *14*

My Sister And Two Brothers, *17*

Free Tickets?, *20*

A Place To Die For, *23*

God's Hand, *27*

Realization, *30*

Reality, *32*

June 2, 2014, *34*

A Little Better Than Heaven, *37*

Sports and Sex, *39*

A Letter, *42*

Names, Names, Names, *46*

Down The Drain, *48*

What A Wedding, *50*

Ducks, *53*

There Are Many Times, *55*

The Restaurant, *58*

The Bird, *61*

Rigoletto—Tragic Comedy, *63*

Joan, *66*

Metropolitan Opera

Roads, *71*

Metropolitan Opera Softball Team, *81*

A Night At The Opera, *83*

A Beauty Of A Story, *85*

Japan, *88*

One Of The Worst Days Of My Life, *89*

Haunting Memories, *92*

Zio Peppino, *95*

Trail Of The Placido Domingo Music, *98*

Conductors, *103*

Prima Donna, *116*

What Do I Write?, *118*

Odds and Ends

John, *123*

Baseball and Music, *126*

Garage Sale, 2008, *127*

A Bumpy Road—A Fantasy, *129*

Give Us This Day Our Daily Bread—A Fiction, *131*

Instructions, *134*

Clouds—A Fantasy, *136*

Speeding—2004, *140*

Things On My Desk, *143*

Something Of A Short Story, *145*

Where Are We Going?, *150*

My Wife's Question—A Fiction, *152*

Stop The Noise, *154*

On And On, *156*

To The Manager Of Starbucks, *158*

Some Silly Thoughts, *160*

Two Characters, *162*

How To Make Your Marriage Better, *163*

About My Friend J.P., *165*

The Pianist—A Fantasy, *167*

There Are Days, *170*

The End, *171*

My Life

AND SO. . .I WAS BORN

M Y MOTHER, FATHER, and their one daughter and two sons came from Italy in the late 1920s. This following story is how I assume that I arrived on the scene. It is very close to what I think happened.

My father was both a musician and a barber. He got a job as a barber, left each morning before 7:00, and came home about 6:30. He also organized a dance band that played at weddings and other affairs, always on weekends. So he was quite busy.

When he came home after cutting hair all day, Mom had dinner waiting for him. She was a great cook, and we always enjoyed the food.

Pop, which is what I called him, would take a bottle of wine from the refrigerator and pour only one glass for the evening. He did so every night except when he was not going to work the next day. For example, on Saturday night he would fill up his glass many times, light a cigar, go for a walk, enjoy the TV, and then go to bed.

In the month of December 1930, Christmas Eve, he as usual had no work the next day. At dinner he filled his glass several times, lit a cigar, went for a walk around the block, came home, and joined Mom who already was in bed.

I was born nine months later.

A PAIN IN THE BUTT

THE OLDER I GET, the more difficult it is to remember things in the past.

However, the other night in bed I remembered the following incident that happened when I was in grammar school. It must have been around seventy-five or so years ago.

PS 85 was two short blocks from my house. Most of the students entered the school from the rear doors. These entrances led to a large area that had a small lunchroom and stairs leading to our classrooms, and contained a twenty-five-foot long, very large bench.

This bench is a bit difficult to describe, but let me try. It was like a regular church pew, and it was as shiny as glass. Almost every day, we boys ran a few steps, jumped on one end of this bench, and then slid down to the other end of it. It was great fun. Sometimes someone would call out, "There's a teacher coming," so we'd all stop.

One day we were doing this so-called ride and it was my turn. I started the short run and the slide. When I got to the end I felt a terrible pain in my rear end. I didn't know what to do. After a short while, and before classes started, I went home.

My mother looked at me and said, "What's wrong with you?" I don't remember what I answered, but she replied, as she always did, "Just wait 'til your father comes home!"

The rest of the day, dealing with that pain, went more slowly than any day of my life.

Pop came home, and she immediately told him that I had hurt myself at school. I took my pants down and he looked at my rear end; for a while, he didn't say a word. Then he grabbed my hand and said, "Let's go." I had no idea what he was going to do. We walked to the subway about three blocks away and got on a train. We took it into Manhattan, got off, and headed to a doctor's office, where I was told to lie down, and within a couple of minutes the doctor had extracted two or three inches of wood from my butt.

We went home; as was his way, my pop didn't talk about this accident. He just looked at me with, I think, some kind of love.

That's all I remember. (But I suspect he probably said to himself, Ah, that's a kid for you.)

GRAMMAR SCHOOL

WHEN I WAS IN GRAMMAR SCHOOL I was known as a bully. I'm sure this term was not used back then. Let me explain why I think I was one. It seemed that I was fighting all the time, and I was good at it. I remember winning every one of those fights—until one memorable day. I was challenged by another boy who was about two or three inches taller than I was and weighed, I'm sure, more than I did.

I don't remember why, but we started fighting. He was getting the best of me, and all of a sudden he had his arms around my neck and was squeezing me. There was nothing I could do. I started to feel like I might be dying. At last he let go, and I fell to the ground. That was a warning that my fighting days should stop.

And there's something else you should know.

I lived, with the rest of my family, in an apartment in a two-story house attached to a similar one. On each side of the complex, walkways led back to garages. Our walkway also led to an empty lot. To get to school, I would go down the walkway and through the lot, cross the street, and I was then in the grammar school yard.

My mother invited her father, my grandfather, to visit us. He was from Italy. He was tall, about six-two, and quite heavy.

One day, after the "holding my neck" fight, walking home from school, I crossed the street and was making my way through the lot. I heard something behind me, turned, and saw five boys trailing me. They were from my school and probably had been in a fight with me at one time or another. I picked up my pace, and they started to run after me. When I got to the end of the lot and close to my walkway, they weren't very far behind.

And there, suddenly, was my grandfather. I ran to him and grabbed him around his knees. The boys stopped. He looked to them like the Frankenstein monster. They ran away. I don't think they ever bothered me again.

I don't remember fighting again in grammar school. I do remember one other time in junior high. It was over some girl I liked and involved some other guy who also liked her. We had a bit of a rumble and, again, I left a loser.

So much for my tough-guy image.

POP

A S WE GET OLDER, many of us get more forgetful about the past. Last night in bed, when I couldn't sleep very well, I started to remember a couple of stories about my father.

He was a barber and a musician. When he came to this country from Italy, he was followed by his four brothers and five sisters. He, and three of his brothers, were barbers. My father also started a dance band, playing at weddings, union affairs, and many other venues. All of these events took place on Saturdays and Sundays.

One of the things I remember is something that happened at a "football wedding." Why was it called that? Because the guest tables were long, and to get food, mostly sandwiches, someone had to toss them to the folks. Food was also given to the members of the band, and my father would come home with his music basket filled with sandwiches, which we used for lunch the following week. (This basket was never used for music and was empty when he left the house.)

Next come bathroom tissues. For many years I never knew

where bathroom tissues came from. I guess I assumed that they were purchased with all other things we needed in our apartment.

One day, I was at the barber shop, getting a quick haircut from my father, when he asked me to take home a package. I did; and when I got home, I looked into it and found a couple of rolls of toilet paper. I figured—and I'm sure I was right—that he got them from the bathroom in the rear of the barber shop. I guess he wanted to save a couple of bucks.

Finally, because my father was a barber, I'd also gotten my first haircut from him. It occurred on a Sunday morning in our kitchen, and that ritual went on for many years. One day, as I was sitting for the usual routine, I said to him, "Pop, don't cut my hair too short."

He said, "Now, I'ma your fadder, and I wanna you to shutuppa when I cutta you hair." From that day on, when I get haircuts from my son, who's also a hair stylist, I never tell him how to do it.

THE SHOT HEARD ROUND THE WORLD—AND IN ASTORIA

IN 1951, I WAS TWENTY YEARS OLD and lived in Astoria, Queens, New York. I was, as I still am, an incredible sports fan. My favorites were always the New York teams—baseball, football, hockey, and basketball.

I don't recall everything that happened in those days, except for something called The Shot Heard Round The World.

This happened in a major league baseball game between the New York Giants and the Brooklyn Dodgers. It was a playoff game, which means that after playing games from late April to the end of September, two teams ended with the exact number of games won and lost. This meant that they had to have a playoff game to determine which team would go to the World Series.

I must describe the area I lived in. It was a street with many different nationalities: Italians, Greeks, Irish, a Polish family, and a couple of others from all around the world. One thing all of us younger guys had in common was that we were either Yankee or

Giant fans. Brooklyn was like another world, and we all thought that no one from our area was their fan.

So when this playoff game took place, we were all rooting for the Giants. For us it was one of the most exciting games in the history of all sports. A Giant player named Bobby Thomson hit a home run to win the game—The Shot Heard Round The World.

I was watching the game in my living room, which faced the street below, and when this happened, within a few minutes, that street was full of screaming, jumping, happy fans. I went down and joined them. We were having the time of our life. All was great, except there was a family that had moved to our street a couple of months before the game who had come from Brooklyn—a father, mother, and two boys. The father and the older son went to work every day, and the younger son, a kid named Nick, about our age, became one of our daily players in the street. Once in a while we would tease him about Brooklyn, but we really got along with him.

While we were all celebrating, many other family members joined us. As we finally started to go back to our houses, someone said, "Where's Nick?" All of us were ready to give him whatever we had left to tease him to the fullest, since he was the only Brooklyn Dodger fan on our street. But no Nick!

As a matter of fact, after this game—and the World Series, which would go into October—not only no Nick, but no other members of the family, were to be seen. Then one night, one of the boys on the street told us that he'd seen Nick go back to his house through the back yard. A person could go to the next street by going down his alley, crossing the parking area, and then going up another alley to get to the next street. This seemed to explain how

Nick used to come and go to school without us seeing him.

As we went through the winter, all returned to normal, and we all looked forward to the spring, the time to enjoy the street and all that spring brings.

And, one day, there was Nick. Honestly we were just happy to see, and play all our games with, him. Once in a while a small, but not hurtful, tease burst forth. The Shot Heard Round The World would remain with most of us the rest of our lives.

DOUBLE TROUBLE

I WAS BORN IN ASTORIA, QUEENS, one of the boroughs of New York City. Between the ages of ten and fifteen, my life revolved around only three things. First, school, which was obligatory; second, music, also obligatory; and third, playing in the street, which at that time was my true love and joy. The games ranged from flipping cards to marbles, stick ball, and one of the street's favorite, slapball. This game is similar to baseball. Bases were marked by chalk in the street; home-plate and first base were on one side of the street, and second and third bases on the other side. Since there weren't that many cars on the street, we never had problems setting up the field.

Teams set up as baseball teams do: first baseman, second baseman, etc. The pitcher would then pitch to the batter, using a rubber ball. He would bounce the ball once to the batter, who would slap it and run, attempting to get on base.

One day double trouble struck.

Playing on the teams were all the boys on the block, which included Italians, Greeks, Irishmen, Frenchmen, and a couple of others. On the opposing team were the famous Irish brothers Matt and Pete Fee, who were very intense and rough. They seemed to be put on Earth just to torment me. They were a bit older than I was and lived directly across the street from me. In those days, I guess the same as today, some bullies existed, and I had been designated by the Fee boys to be bullied. This bullying stopped when my cousins, all five of them, who lived in the Bronx and visited us about once a month, found out about it, confronted the Fee brothers, and told them to lay off or else. It worked.

Back to the slap-ball game. It was moving ahead in the usual great way when—I can't remember the exact details, but there was a close play, and one of the Fee boys tagged me, and I banged my ankle against the curb and fell to the ground in great pain. Some of the players told me to stop being a baby and get up and start playing again. When I stood up, I immediately fell again and told them I had to go home. As I crawled up one flight to our apartment, I was met by my mom. She yelled out, "What's wrong?"

I told her that I had hurt myself and wasn't feeling well. She told me to go to my room and added, as I have already said she always did, "Wait until your father comes home!"

Oy! Pop left each morning around 6:30. He was a barber and had to perform a couple of shaves on executives in the garment district of Manhattan. He usually came home around 7:00 p.m. He was exhausted and looked forward to a couple of glasses of wine and the usual great meal Mom would have prepared.

Coming up the stairs, he was greeted by Mom, who immediately said something like, "You should see your son!"

He found me in some corner of the apartment and asked, "What the hell is going on?"

I told him that I had been playing outside and hurt my ankle. I was still in great pain, but he acted as if his whole life was falling apart. He tried to get some more details about what had happened. As I fumbled about, I mentioned that the Fee boys were involved. He turned to me said, "Didn't I tell you never to play with the Fee boys?" followed by a blow to my head.

Later that night, I was in the hospital with a broken ankle. A few weeks later, I was out of the hospital with a cast from just below my knee to my toes. A few days more, with the cast still on, I was again playing in the street, except, when the Fee boys came, I left. I did not want any more double trouble.

MY SISTER AND TWO BROTHERS

MY MOTHER AND FATHER were both born in 1896, in Bari, Italy, and married in 1914. My sister, Mary, a gorgeous gal, was born in 1915. My father, Frank, went into the army in 1915, just before she was born. He didn't see her until he returned from the Army in 1918. My brother Tony was born in 1919, and my brother Joe in 1920. I was born in 1931...but that's another story.

The first thing I remember about my sister is her holding me in her arms when I was a baby. How I can remember this is a mystery to me. I was told later that Mary, since she was sixteen when I was born, took care of me most of the time.

I will leave the most memorable incident that I experienced with her for my last chapter.

Tony was the only sibling who did not have any musical talent; however, he was an excellent commercial artist and always had a good position wherever he worked. When he was drafted into the army, he used his skills by helping to make maps and things related to the military. He ended his service while he was in Italy. He had married Marian while in the army, before he went overseas. When he returned, they had three boys.

He became the first son of my father to forego a custom that went on in our family for as long as most of us could remember—naming children after grandfathers, grandmothers, and then from the grandfather of the father to the grandparents of the mother. In those days, having eight or more children made this method of naming children useful.

Tony's first son was named Frank, after my father. His second son was named Ronald, however—a totally non-Italian name—and his youngest son Rick, again not traditional. But who really cared?

My brother Joe was a jazz musician, and he and I were really wonderful friends. I started to learn many things about music from him, which of course included jazz. When Joan and I found a house in New Jersey that was quite expensive, we asked both Tony and Joe to come and see the house before we made the final decision to purchase it. Tony said we were crazy to buy such an expensive house, but Joe said, "It's great—go ahead and get it." That, and many other things coming from Joe, kept us close. When he went into the army, he started a jazz band that played for the troops in England. When the war was over, he came home, married, got a day job, and played events on week-ends with my father and others.

Joe and Helena, his wife, had a real tragedy in their lives. Their son Bobby was killed in Vietnam. Helena died a few years later. Many of us felt she'd died of a broken heart. It took a long time for Joe to recover, but he did and lived well into his eighties. I got along with him very well, and years after that tragedy he moved to California, where I visited him and my sister Mary, who lived close to him. When I wasn't with him, I would speak to him on the phone at least once a week. Our conversations always started with him asking for a joke, so I was always prepared. The last time I went out West, he was not in good health and died a few days after I arrived. I was glad I was there to attend his funeral.

My sister was also a reason I spent some time out West. She was not in good health either and passed away in her early nineties. I got along with her so very well, and I will never forget sitting with her and asking, "Mary, you don't go to church, but do you believe in God?"

She told me, "Of course I believe in God. Just look into a mirror and look at your face, and then think of the people you have seen in your lifetime. How many of them look exactly like you? Think of your insides...how could this have happened? God certainly was involved. Think of your brain. Again, God had to have something to do with it. I could go on and on, thinking about what God has created, and never have any doubt. Yes, I do believe in God."

Now, many years after my sister and my two brothers passed away, I think of them frequently—and these little stories will always be with me.

FREE TICKETS?

I T WAS A COLD WINTER NIGHT. I was about twenty years old and had two guys I hung out with—John S., a clarinet student who never played very well, and Sal Cuneo, a free-lance trombonist who was very talented and played in the New York area.

John S. lived in Brooklyn, and Sal lived in Queens. We would get in touch with each other during the week and make plans to meet, usually on week-ends. We went to some concerts, movies, and other events if the cost was not too steep, since none of us had much money. Most of the time we met in Manhattan to do our thing.

I had a former clarinet teacher then who was playing in the Boston Symphony. I made plans to hear them at Carnegie Hall. When I called to tell him I was going, he said he'd have free tickets for me I could pick up backstage. I met my two friends and got the envelope with the tickets. When I opened it, there were only two.

What to do?

We couldn't afford to buy another ticket, so we decided to hang around near the box office and ask if someone had an extra ticket.

We were not having any luck, so we talked it over again and decided that, since the three of us couldn't go to the concert, maybe we could sell the two. I was appointed to try and sell them while John S. and Sal waited nearby. I first stood near the entrance and asked people, as they passed by, if they wanted to buy a couple of tickets. No response. I then went near the box office and again asked.

All of a sudden, a hand touched me on the shoulder and said, "You are under arrest—and call your friends over."

It was a uniformed policeman. As I heard these words, my world came apart. Visions of my father and prison flashed before me. I called the guys over. The policeman told the three of us to leave the building. He then said, "I know you guys, always trying to sell tickets. I want you to walk in front of me to the police station."

In the frigid weather, arrested and shaking like a leaf, we trudged off to the precinct. One of us started to put his hands in his pockets. The policeman barked, "Keep your hands outside where I can see 'em!"

The station was about four blocks away, and when we got there we were ushered into a room and told to wait until he returned.

It was at least an hour before he did. When he came in, he told us that we were not the ticket scalpers he'd thought we were, and that we were allowed to leave. He said that, even though we were breaking the law, the sergeant was being very nice to let us go. However, didn't we think that a small gift to the sergeant was in order?

We looked at each other, not really knowing what kind of gift he had in mind. Maybe a TV? How about a free haircut by my father? We stared at him, puzzled. He told us to think about it, and that he would return in a short while. He did return and said, "Well?" Again we were confused. He then said, "How about a saw-buck?" and left again. A sawbuck! I think Sal finally said that that was twenty-five dollars. We were in such a hurry to get out of there that we put all our money together, leaving enough for the subway to get us home. We came up with about eighteen dollars. When the policeman came back, we handed the money to him, and he said we could leave.

We drew some conclusions from all this: First, never try to sell tickets; second, never go to Carnegie Hall again (this one we didn't follow); and third, always have gloves when it's cold.

I haven't seen or heard from John S. or Sal in over sixty years.

A PLACE TO DIE FOR

YEARS AGO I TRAVELED all over the world, sometimes with the Metropolitan Opera. We went to Japan, England, France, Italy, and Germany. What a treat—and all for free.

Since I was often in the traveling mood and my wife, Joan, only came along on these trips once in a while, we also traveled on our own. We went to Italy a few times, a wondrous place, with plenty of delicious food and lots of places to see. We also traveled out West.

One day at work a fellow musician, Dennis, came into my office and told me that he had just bought a house near his folks in a place near Estes Park, Colorado, at the foot of the Rocky Mountains. He asked me if I'd like to visit him there. Before he could finish the sentence, I said yes. The available date was a week before he would get there, but he said we could stay at the house until he arrived.

I went home and told Joan, who, even in the middle of preparing supper, was ready to go. Dennis gave me all the instructions to get to his place, and we made our plans.

We took a plane to Denver, rented a car, and started the trip of a couple of hours. It was late in the day. As we followed the instructions, it started to get darker. One of the signs we were supposed to look for was an old Indian totem pole. After missing this pole a few times, we finally found it and turned onto a dirt road. By then, it was already dark.

After about one mile, we saw the house. I had been told that the key was under the front doormat. At first I couldn't find it and had a bit of a panic. But I located the key, and Joan and I got our luggage and entered a rustic home that was wonderfully comfortable. We went up to the bedroom and, after a short time, fell asleep.

We were awakened by sunshine, found a large door that led from the bedroom to a balcony, opened the door, and almost fell over at the most beautiful sight we had ever seen—mountains, trees in a host of shades, and a brook. It was fantastic!

We spent the next few days seeing all we could. We took a trip into the Rocky Mountains and spent a few days walking around downtown Estes Park. We ate in many wonderful restaurants and had a great time.

Dennis appeared a few days later and he took us to other interesting places.

A day or so after that, another musician friend from the Met Opera came, and Dennis suggested that we all go to a place called Peaceful Valley for a bite. We got there, parked the car, went into the restaurant, and had a hearty and enjoyable lunch.

Joan and I didn't have either the time or the foresight to ask more about the place or do more than glance around. It looked like some kind of resort.

The trip ended, and we went home with a bagful of wonderful things to tell our friends and family.

Two years later, I asked Dennis about visiting him again. He told me that he had sold the house. Since we wanted to go back anyway, I asked him if he could recommend a place for us to stay. He said there was a motel nearby with a vacancy sign and gave me the phone number; I made a reservation for Joan, me, and my son John, who was living on the West Coast and planned to meet us at the airport.

We took the plane to Denver, met him, rented a car, and drove off to the motel. We already knew the area, and finding the motel was not a problem; the problem was seeing the rooms. They were horrible. Without getting into details, we stayed about five minutes and left.

What to do?

We headed for Estes Park, the largest small town nearby. We found an information center and asked for places to stay. Almost all the hotels were full. We were told of a place about twenty-five miles away. We had no choice, so we got in the car and headed for this unknown place. As we were driving, all of us a bit uneasy and unhappy, we passed the restaurant where Dennis had taken us for lunch, Peaceful Valley. I stopped the car and said, "Let's go and see if they have rooms for us—what have we got to lose?"

Peaceful Valley is an old-fashioned dude ranch. You book your rooms, usually for a week or more, get all your meals, and enjoy the many activities.

They did have rooms for us. We were overjoyed, mostly because of finding any place—and our rooms were wonderful.

Meals were served family style at big long tables, sitting next to people you were meeting for the first time; evening entertainment included square dancing, which we had never done before; and during the week there was a rodeo show. They had an indoor swimming pool, since it always got rather cool each night, and, believe it, horseback riding, which was a first for me.

My son and I signed up for that adventure. We were told to go to the stable and pick a horse. We did so, and were next told to go to a large barn. There an instructor first told us how to mount and dismount the horses. He then led us, in the barn, around and around, he walking and us riding. This lesson lasted well over an hour.

The next day was the big test. About ten or so of us "cowboys" gathered and were taken for our first ride outside the barn.

It was wonderful. The next couple of days, we rode horses. Joan did not join us. Being originally from Brooklyn, she said that no one from Brooklyn rides horses. That was okay with us.

On the third day, we were taken on horseback up a mountain to a chapel. Riding a horse up and down the side of a mountain was another incredible adventure.

It was one of the most enjoyable and beautiful places I have ever been in my life. The name says it all: Peaceful Valley.

Whenever I have a problem getting to sleep, I envision that place and, before you know it, it's morning.

GOD'S HAND

Today is Friday. Yesterday, April 24, 2008, I had quite a day. But before I tell you about it, permit me to describe the events leading up to it.

When I retired about seven years earlier, one of the things I had done was join the Senior Center Services in Teaneck, New Jersey. I had first been interested in joining the Men's Fitness Class. It was held three times a week: Tuesdays, Thursdays, and Fridays. This class started at 12:15 p.m. and lasted about an hour. I then found out that the Seniors Services had many different classes: bingo, dance, painting, yoga, and on and on. I signed up for a discussion class and a writing class. . .one of my favorites.

During that period, our writing teacher could not continue, so a couple of us decided to muddle on without her.

At one of the men's fitness classes I met a fellow named Abbott and told him about this informal writers' arrangement. He asked if he could join us. We all welcomed him.

One Tuesday morning, I had many personal chores to take care of and missed the writing class, which ran from 10:00 to 11:00 a.m.

When I showed up for the 12:15 fitness class, Abbott asked me why I hadn't come to the writing class. He had read a story he had written years before. I told him why, and I noticed that he was holding some sheets in his hand and asked him if that was the story he had read. He said it was. I asked him if I could take it home with me and return it when I saw him at the fitness class the following Thursday. He agreed but told me it was the only copy he had.

On Thursday I wanted to bring piles of cardboard, cans, and newspapers to the town recycling center. I went there about 10:30 a.m., then went home and had lunch, and left for the men's fitness group.

As I entered the gym, I saw Abbott and froze. What had happened to his story? I could only think that I had wrapped it up with everything else and trundled it off to Recycling. I immediately left the gym and went back to the recycling center. When I got there, I found two attendants eating lunch, chicken parmesan sandwiches. I told them what had happened, and they both said they would help me find my wrapped newspapers as soon as they had finished their lunch.

I jumped into the pile, which by then was enormous. Talk about finding a needle in a haystack. After about twenty minutes, the two attendants joined me. One went into the deep end of the pile and, with the other helping him, got his foot stuck under what looked like ten piles of newspapers. He needed my help to get out. Finally I saw a pile that looked familiar. I quickly opened it and looked and looked without spotting the story.

We continued looking for close to an hour and finally gave up.

The two attendants felt almost as badly as I did.

I returned to the adult center just as the gym class was ending, looked for Abbott, and told him that I had lost his story. He was dejected, in no way feeling worse than I.

It was just 1:00 p.m.; I had a meeting at 1:30. I thought I'd say hello to a friend at the center, Kathy, who is the nurse. Feeling as I did, I asked her to take my blood pressure. While she was doing this, I told her what had happened. She said to me, "John, my family has lost two important things in our lives, and by praying to Saint Anthony, they found both of these items."

I said to myself, What have I got to lose by praying? and offered up a prayer immediately.

I went to my meeting, got into my car, said a couple more prayers to Saint Anthony, and drove home. When I got there, my wife was in her computer room, and I told her my problem. As I was talking to her, she looked out the window into the backyard, pointed to the bench where I had been reading the story, and said, "Go take a look." I ran out, and there it was!

So Thursday, April 24, 2008, was one of the worst days of my life. But thanks to Saint Anthony, my wife, Kathy, and the two attendants, my problem was resolved. I was most relieved to hand the story to Abbott. The next day I gave bottles of wine to Kathy and the two attendants.

Coincidentally, last Saturday, April 19, my brother passed away. His name was Anthony. Perhaps he too had been in on the solution.

REALIZATION

I STARTED PLAYING THE CLARINET in PS 85 grammar school at the age of eight. After two years I went to JHS 141. By then I had started to understand music. This included a bit of classical music, jazz (which my brother played), and many technical details.

My first week in junior high, all the students were called to a very large auditorium to be greeted by the principal. We were told to start by singing the national anthem. A short while into the singing, I saw, out of the corner of my eye, a teacher walking up and down the aisles. She stopped at the end of the aisle where I was standing and looked down it. She put one finger on her lips. I didn't stop, because I wasn't sure who she was signaling. She walked away. We all continued to sing, but in a very short time she was again at the end of our aisle—and trying to get my attention. When I spotted her, she pointed at me and, with her hands, signaled me to stop singing. I did.

When we were all excused and told to go to our classrooms, I found her and asked her why she'd wanted me to stop singing. My world almost crashed when she said, "You have a very unpleasant voice."

Ever after that, my career concentrated on the clarinet, and I have always sung very softly.

It was a day of realization.

REALITY

REALITY AND VISUAL OBSERVATION can be so incredibly different. I am talking about seeing the same incident both in person and on television or on the movie screen.

Ever since the advent of television and movies, certain stories have been in the eyes of the world. For example, before these two technologies, how many people ever saw a person being shot or knifed to death? We have gone a long way since to explore these ways of killing. We started first with movies made about the Depression, when gangsters shot their enemies. These murders were pretty simple—a car drives up the street and a couple thugs open their windows and tommy-gun down the bad or good guys. Not much blood, but was this enough? Not at all; we have now progressed to where we can see rivers of blood, parts of the body cut off, knives in all parts of the body and on and on.

What progress!

There is a TV channel that presents boxing. Not only do they show the sport of boxing, but they seem to pray that one of the combatants gets a cut on his face. Now they can't seem to wait for the bell to ring. Once it does, the cameras pan directly to the cut. As the trainers work on it, the camera gets closer and closer. What a wonderful thrill to see all this blood.

Television has even brought us operations being performed by surgeons. More blood!

I have to admit that I watched boxing on television a while back. It didn't bother me that much. One day I went to see a live match. To see two guys hit each other, to see the ever- present blood, was a real shock.

I have never seen a murder, never seen a person immediately after being murdered, so I guess I'm missing something. I hope, in what time I have left, I never do.

This all came to my mind a few days ago when I called my son to say hello. I sensed that something was wrong from the way he was talking. He said he was fine, but that same morning, when he was going to work in lower Manhattan, something had happened to him that he had probably seen hundreds of times on television or in the movies—a man had jumped out of building and landed very close to him. He didn't know the guy, and had no idea of the circumstances, but he was profoundly affected.

Maybe the immature images we see on the screens are not as real as they really are. That's a good thing.

JUNE 2, 2014

I HAD A 10:00 A.M. APPOINTMENT with a doctor about three minutes away from my home by car. I got there at 9:45 and, as usual,
sat down and waited to be called.

About 10:20 my cell phone rang. It was my son Mickey. He told
me that he had just received a call from the police that my house
alarm was ringing, and that he was on his way to my house to see
what was going on.

A couple of seconds later, the nurse called my name and took
me in to see the doctor. I did so and called my son, who by then was
in my house with about four police cars outside. I waited in a
quandary. The doctor finally came in, did what he had to do, and I
rushed out at about 11:00.

When I got home, the police cars were still there, and I went
through the back door leading to the kitchen. I found my son and
six policemen.

They told me not to touch anything. There was broken glass
on the floor at the back door and, most incredibly, a hammer that

was not mine lay on the kitchen counter.

They took me to the stairway going upstairs, where they showed me some jewelry on the steps. When we reached Joan's room, I saw many other pieces on the floor.

Joan was away and would be returning sometime that afternoon.

The police were doing an incredible search of everything, looking for clues.

They put the hammer in a paper bag. They took fingerprints of many places.

Finally, after asking me if I had any ideas who might have buggerized my house, they gave me a phone number to call if I had any possible ideas.

My wife and I reviewed the possibilities.

A few years before, we had hired a couple of young fellows to do work on the outside of our house. Once in a while, I asked them to do some chores that weren't part of their normal routine; for this I would always give them a tip. One day I was introduced to another young man who would be joining them. He was a tell guy and seemed somewhat odd. At the end of last summer, I asked two of them, including the tall one, to bring two very heavy lounges into the house from the back yard. One went into the downstairs den, and the other had to be carried upstairs to Joan's bedroom. This bedroom was where Joan kept a tray with many pieces of jewelry. The men did their chore and all went fine.

Joan and I started to put together all that happened on June 2. Our door to the kitchen has a four-part window. Each pane is three-and-a-half by five-and-a-half inches.

We always put on our alarm when we go out and when we go up to sleep. I had put on the alarm when I went to the doctor's office. Someone broke one of the small panes with a hammer, put his arm though the door, and opened it from the inside. He then started to go to the stairs leading to the bedroom. He had been there when he took the chair up.

On the felon's way to that room, the alarm went off. He must have panicked, because he dropped many pieces of jewelry on the bedroom floor and on the way down the steps. Then he went out the back door. He left his hammer on the kitchen counter, where he'd put it to start with.

I offered this theory to the sergeant.

We have spoken to, and had meetings with, the police department about ten times, with no results.

Life goes on!

A LITTLE BETTER THAN HEAVEN

SINCE I HAVE NOT BEEN to heaven, this is a story about a place in Italy that has to be as close to heaven as I can imagine.

My wife and I went on a trip to Italy years ago with the Perillo tour company. We traveled by bus from city to city— living in the best accommodations in wonderful hotels, ate great food in superb restaurants, and enjoyed other lovely advantages, like not getting up too early. The bus rides were also slow enough so we could see everything we wanted to, even if we did not stop many times.

We had no idea what Sicily was going to be like. However, Joan's family came from a city in that part of Italy, so she and I were excited to see where her family had originated.

Since Sicily is a very large island off the very bottom of Italy, we had to take a boat to get there. When we disembarked, busses were waiting for us. We started up the mountainside and stopped at Taormina. Once off the bus, we looked back down to the mountains and the sea. Wow! It was beautiful. The food and the hotel were excellent, too.

In a day or so, the guide told us that we would be going on a walking tour of the city. We saw old buildings, churches, and many great places to eat. We walked for quite a while and enjoyed every step.

Then we approached a large section that looked to be in ruins. As we got closer, we learned that it was an open-air theatre built by the Greeks a few thousand years ago. It was called Teatro Griego De Taormina, or Greek Theatre of Taormina. (The Greeks must have controlled Sicily then.)

Many of us on the tour, and many other sightseers, went inside. We took our time and enjoyed every minute in that ancient place. Ahead of us steps led up to where people sat to watch performances then. We were told that shows are still performed there.

Then something unique happened: Where was Joan? I looked around from where I was sitting and all up and down that very large area. Where was she?

Then, I heard a voice coming from the stage way down the steps. She was singing. All the people around us, and I, imagined that all in the theatre of that bygone time had stopped and listened.

She was singing one of the most beautiful arias ever written. It was from Puccini's Madam Butterfly, "Un Bel Di" (A Beautiful Day).

When she finished, the crowd went wild and applauded for quite a long while. I went down, gave her a kiss, looked up at the sky, and said to myself, "I hope heaven will be like today."

SPORTS AND SEX

I WAS BORN AND RAISED in Astoria, which is part of Queens, New York. We lived on a street which was home to families of many different nationalities. There were Italians, Greeks, Jews, Irish, one Polish family, and a couple of others. Everybody seemed to have large families. It looked to me as if there were none with fewer than three children.

Since there were so many kids without TVs and other things to do, we spent most of our time after school playing together. First it was marbles, then flipping cards, then stoop-ball, then street slap-ball and then, the best of all, stick-ball in the middle of the street.

Since there were not as many cars as today, traffic was not such a problem. Someone would yell, "Car coming"; we would stop, and after it passed, we would continue. (I'm sure today that would be impossible in these same streets.)

So, after school, we headed to the street.

About two short blocks away was a school with a large play-ground. There were two places to play softball. So, many of us, instead of playing on our street, went to this schoolyard to play. As time went on, more and more kids came to play. We had to find a way to organize all those who came, and I got involved in that. Without getting into many, many details that happened in organizing, I started a betting game. Every player had to put up fifty cents for each game. The winning players got back one dollar each.

Winning the game was fun, but winning one dollar was great.

OK—now, after a long time, here is what happened one day.

I was on a team that was losing 2 to 1 in the last inning. We were the last up at bat. There were two outs and one base runner, and I was at bat. I hit one of the best balls of my life and started running. The base runner, already on base, came home to tie the game. I was running like mad and, just as I got to home base, the ball arrived. I was safe. My team went crazy. I sat down and tried to catch my breath. I was alright. All collected their dollar and left, except for me and one other player.

In a couple of minutes we left too and headed to the candy store that many of us went to after each game. I ordered my favorite, Mission Orange soda, sat down on a stool facing the counter, and enjoyed time with my friends. As I was drinking, other customers were coming in and out of the store. All of a sudden the door opened, and I saw the most beautiful girl I had ever seen. Some of the guys took a quick look and went back to kidding with each other, but I could not take my eyes off her. She seemed to be looking for some item and was strolling slowly around the shelves in the glass cases. She was coming closer, of course not paying any attention to me. She stopped a few feet from me and started to look at some items on a shelf next to me.

Then she bent down to see something on the bottom shelf.

Oh, Lord. My first look at the most beautiful breasts in the world....

My first sex!

The real end of this story is that I never got to first base with her.

A LETTER

THIS LETTER WAS WRITTEN on September 24, 1971, to the Daily News, which had a section called "Jolt Index." Letters to this department told stories about streets in New York City—potholes and sidewalks needing repair, broken curbs, and so on.

> *Dear Sir:*
>
> *I have been reading your, "Jolt Index" articles and have enjoyed their humor. However, whenever you drive over some of these roads that you write about, it's not so funny.*
>
> *I would like to relate a true story about my own street.*
>
> *About three years ago the curbing in front of our house, and a neighbor's house, started to fall apart. The street was already potholed and would have registered at 90 on your meter, which goes up to 100. Very soon it was starting to look like the*

Grand Canyon.

My wife and I started writing letters to all departments that we imagined might help in getting our street repaired, including a Mr. Fixit in the Long Island Press and a few TV personalities interested at that time in these situations. We got to know our local assemblyman and peppered him with requests to have our street fixed. Many inspectors visited our street during this period, but the road only got worse.

Finally on Thursday, October 28, 1971, an army of about forty men (which included thirty-eight foremen) and four trucks arrived on our street. After they sized up the street and informed the inhabitants that they would start working on it the next day, they left two trucks behind and departed.

Early the next day they reappeared. My wife was so excited that she had coffee waiting for them. After their coffee break, during which a few workers who didn't drink coffee used our front lawn water hose for drinking water, they then proceeded to sweep the autumn leaves off the street. After this, they left.

Monday was a Catholic Holiday. . . . No work!

Tuesday was Election Day. . . . No work!

Wednesday brought a promise of great things to come. Early (ten a.m.), a load of hot tar arrived, was dumped onto the street, leveled out, run over by a giant press, and a section of about forty-by-two feet was a joy for all of us to see. After lunch. . .they all left.

The next day, Thursday, was pay day. . . . No work!

Friday started off with a bang and ended with an even larger bang. A rather large section of the street, and two sections of the broken curbing, were repaired early in the day. All this time we had been told to move our cars away from our street. Many of us had parked at the end of the street, which is at the bottom of a hill.

A little after lunch, one of the large tar trucks had trouble with its brakes. That might have been OK except that this happened when the truck was in the middle of the block and had no driver. The ensuing bang completely destroyed one car and did enough damage to another that it could not be removed for months.

This not only shook up all the neighbors but also the workers, who then took the rest of the day off. (By this time my wife had stopped serving coffee and I'd shut off the water hose.)

This incident and many others—including the disappearance of all the workers and trucks for about two weeks, rain, snow, holidays, and special events dragged this on close to Christmas.

Our street is approximately five hundred feet

long. I'm sure if one figured the number of streets that are in need of repair, multiplied by the number of crews doing this type of work in New York City, they might come up with the completion date around the year 5000. Of course the streets might be made of gold by then, so who cares.

NAMES, NAMES, NAMES

M Y NAME IS JOHN GRANDE. I've always been called John except when I was a child. Then I was sometimes called "Johnny." That's it!

When I met my wife, her name was Joan Sena. Sometimes "Joanie," and sometimes, using her middle name, Joan Kathleen Sena or Joan K. Sena. That was it.

When we got married, she changed her name to Joan Grande. It remained that way for years.

Then she decided to find a way to use her maiden name. She came up with Joan Sena Grande. Okay. Sena looks like a middle name to most people. What happens when you spell it this way, Joan Sena-Grande? Is her last name Sena-Grande? Also other variations, Joan S. Grande, Joan Kathleen Sena-Grande, Joan K. Sena-Grande. I could go on for a couple more pages.

Actually this has resulted in all kinds of problems. Doctors don't know who is showing up; pharmacists don't get the prescription correct; insurance policies and Medicare letters are confused, and on and on.

What's going on? I sometimes am not even sure to whom I'm married.

DOWN THE DRAIN

JOAN, MY WIFE, told me one day that she was pregnant. We were in our third year of marriage and were really looking forward to our first child. She said her doctor had recommended the Lamaze system for us to attend before the baby arrived, so that we could practice a relaxing way to make the delivery less painful. We agreed to go.

The weekly sessions were easy to follow. They included breathing, positions, and other ways to make the delivery a more positive experience. I went to all the sessions and looked forward to the delivery day, when I would also be in the delivery room.

When the night arrived and Joan began to have contractions, we went to the hospital and were set up near the delivery room to wait.

But her pains didn't go as expected. It was taking too long, and the doctor came in, said he would help the progress move along, and gave her a quick whiff of a gas to relax her. In a short while, she was ready, and they moved her to the delivery room. I followed her and got dressed like a nurse. I stood next to her and held her hand.

The delivery again started going rather slowly, so the doctor told the anesthetist to come close to Joan and be ready to apply anesthesia. He stood on her left while I stood on her right.

Then everything I had looked forward to evaporated.

The anesthesiologist, distracted by the doctor, put the mask near me. I inhaled the gas and reeled backward toward the door, trying to recover. While I was doing this, Mickey, our son, was born.

All the months of sex, all the months of waiting, down the drain!

About three years later, Joan was again pregnant. When I took her to the hospital that time, I got her to her room, went downstairs to the waiting room, closed my eyes, and took a nap.

I was awakened by the doctor, who told me that I had my second son.

That was easy!

WHAT A WEDDING

I HAVE MADE MANY TRIPS overseas both with the Metropolitan Opera and with my wife. I have been to Italy, Germany, England, France, Canada, Japan, and Spain.

There were many wonderful things to see in all these countries, and many small incidents occurred.

I was in my office in New York when a nice gentleman came and asked for a music score. I got it for him and asked, because of his accent, where he was from. He told me he was Italian and came from a town near Venice. I told him I was going to Italy with my wife and might get to Venice. He said if we did go there to be sure to go to a restaurant around the corner from the opera house. He gave me the name of the place. I said I would certainly remember what he told me.

Arriving in Venice, and seeing that many of the streets were actually waterways, was of course incredible. Even though we had known they were, seeing them in person is something I cannot easily describe.

So Joan and I started to walk from our hotel toward the opera house, asking directions along the way. It was exhilarating. Finally we found ourselves in a piazza facing the opera house. On one side there was a large indoor-outdoor restaurant and many other stores. Since this was late morning, I asked Joan if she thought any rehearsals might be going on. We went into the lobby, found a person in the ticket area, and asked her. She told us that one was. When I told her that I was from the Metropolitan Opera, she said that we could go to the backstage entrance and might be able to speak to someone about seeing the rehearsal. We did, and a wonderful man, after seeing my Met ID card, invited us in and asked if we would like to see the rehearsal. "Yes!" I exclaimed.

He opened a door, and we walked in and sat in the last row. The opera was Lohengrin. I had heard this music many times and knew it was the act with the wedding march, which has been played millions of times all over the world.

Joan and I were truly enjoying the music. The wedding march was quickly approaching. This particular production had a hundred-person chorus backstage, and when the music started for the march, they began to come onstage. When about half of them had entered, the conductor yelled out, in Italian with a German accent, "Stop! Stop!"

They all did. He called the chorus master out and yelled at him about something that was wrong. They all went back and started again. Once again, he stopped them and again yelled at the chorus master. By this time, Joan and I had started to giggle. Again the chorus went back and started over, and again the conductor yelled. We were in hysterics and we had to leave. Once outside, we let loose with unending laughter.

Finally we decided to find a place to have lunch. I remembered the man telling me about the restaurant up the street from the opera house, and we easily found it. We went and had a wonderful meal. The waiter, who spoke a bit of English, told us that the place was part of the one in the piazza, but the prices were much more reasonable.

So we had a good meal, saved a few bucks, and hoped to never hear the wedding march again.

DUCKS

I HAVE A POOL in my back yard, and for years some ducks have been flying by and leaving as soon as someone comes outside.

About three weeks ago I looked at an area near the pool, which was covered with red mulch and saw an egg. I took it to my wife, and we thought that some creature had laid it.

A couple of days later, I saw one of the ducks that used to fly by sitting in the spot where I had seen the egg. When I got close, she flew away, and I then saw four more eggs. The next morning she was back and sitting on her eggs. I very quietly crept close to her, and she stayed there. Each day I got a bit closer, and she sort of got used to me. A few days later, when she went into the pool for some water, I looked and saw nine eggs. Wow!

She did not leave her eggs even when many of us got close to her. When it started to get dark, she covered the eggs with the mulch and flew away. (She probably went to a local bar for a bit to eat and a couple of beers.) On Father's Day I had my family over, about ten people, and she didn't move away from her eggs all day.

Someone looked up information on a computer and said that the eggs might be there about three weeks. We couldn't wait. Hopefully the baby ducks would go for a swim in our pool.

IT'S ALL OVER!

When I went outside, the duck was gone, and the eggs were broken and all over the yard. That's the end.

What a shame!

THERE ARE MANY TIMES

THERE ARE MANY TIMES when I think of my mother and father. However, the older I get, the less I remember about them. Here's one story I can't ever forget.

My father was a wonderful guy and treated me, the last of four children, born about ten years after my brother, very nicely. He had a few rules that were not hard to follow. As I got a bit older he told me that I should be home at a certain time if I should be out with friends or, when I entered my late teens, with a girl.

While I was still a student at the Juilliard School of Music, I was playing with an orchestra in Brooklyn that performed opera about once a month. One day, the manager asked me if I would like to go on a tour with the orchestra for about six weeks. Since I was graduating soon, I accepted the offer. The tour would be starting in September. The opera was *Madam Butterfly*. All went well, and after about three rehearsals we took off.

There was a mixture of musicians, male and female. After a week, I took the oboe player, a girl, out for a drink. It was the beginning of my first affair. Without getting into all the details, it was great. I had quite a time for that month and a half. When the tour ended, we returned to New York and our homes and families.

Since the oboe player lived in Manhattan, I saw her a couple of times a week. We went out for dinner, a movie, or just stayed in her apartment. I had a car and always looked at my watch to make sure I left her early enough that my father wouldn't get upset.

One night, one of the greatest of my life, I forgot to look at my watch. I eventually dressed, got behind the wheel, and started the drive home from Manhattan to Queens, speeding as much as I could.

When I got to the bridge, I kept speeding. About halfway across, I looked into my rear mirror and saw a police car right behind me. I slowed down, and when we got to the other side of the bridge, the policeman directed me to the curb, climbed out of his car, came up to my open window, and said, "Do you know you were speeding?"

I was in a bit of shock and didn't answer him.

"Didn't you hear me?" he asked.

"Officer," I said, "I'm really sorry that I was speeding, but if I don't get home soon, my father will kill me for being out so late."

He stared at me a minute for a bit before saying, "OK, get going—but *do not speed.*"

I was both relieved and nervous driving the last ten minutes to get home. I parked the car on the street in front of the apartment and got out. It was dark. I quietly got my keys out and went up a couple of steps to the front door. After I opened the door, I removed my shoes, because I had to walk up one flight to get to the apartment. I slowly crept to my room. I sat on the bed in complete silence, took my clothes off, got into bed, and listened for any noise but heard only silence.

The next morning my father had already left for work, and my mother did not say a word about the previous night.

Sixty-five years later, I still remember the meaning of that silence.

THE RESTAURANT

WHEN I WAS IN MY LATE TEENS and still in school, I got a job as a waiter in an Italian restaurant called Savoia in Manhattan on Third Avenue between Thirty-second and Thirty-third Streets.

It was a somewhat small place and seemed to be busy most of the time.

They had a bar with a bartender, a wonderful cook, and a bus boy, José, who did many chores.

José, besides helping the cook and cleaning dishes, was also the bouncer whenever a problem occurred at the bar. He would help the bartender straighten out most guys who had had too much to drink.

One night, José was called to the bar to deal with a really loud guy. He asked him to leave, to no avail. So he took him by the arms and dragged him outside. I was serving someone and saw what happened. In the next minute or so, I heard some screaming and ran out. There was José on top of the guy, punching him. I immediately grabbed José by the arms and pulled him off.

He was steaming. He told me that the drunk just didn't want to leave and had tried to punch him, and that that was why he'd done what he had. In another couple of minutes, the man got up and walked away.

First, a bit of back ground on the next story. I knew there were gay people in the world, but I had never met one or understood much about them. One night two men came into the restaurant and sat down in one of the booths. I asked them if they would like to have a drink. One of them said, "Two martinis."

I went to the bar, got the drinks, and took them to the booth. As I turned around to attend another table, the man said, "Excuse me, young feller. If these drinks don't taste as they should, I will throw them on you." As he said it, he waved his hand in a very effeminate way.

He took a sip and waved to me that all was OK. José, who was watching and hearing what was going on, said, "Forget what just happened. Queers are always making a problem."

This was my first introduction to homosexuals; I found later in life that they are no more a problem than most other people.

And finally the incident that I hope I will have a chance to tell St. Peter, so that my entrance to heaven will be a bit easier.

One evening an older couple came in and went directly to a booth. The woman had on a dress that touched the top of her shoes. The man moved to the left side of the table (as you faced them) and slid in, and the woman took her place on the other side.

They immediately ordered a couple of drinks. In a few minutes, as I passed them, they ordered another drink, which I quickly served. They were ready to order. They both wanted a salad, and gave me their main course orders. They also asked me to bring them another drink.

When the main courses were ready, I took them to the table and asked if I should take away the salad dishes, which were not finished. They told me to leave them there. I put the main course dishes in front of them.

While I was doing this, the man started to slide out from his seat and, with his feet still on the floor, leaned his left hand on the corner of the table. He asked, "Where is the men's room?"

I half turned and pointed. "Down that small hallway." He rose, leaning on that left hand…and then it happened, one of the funniest things in my life. The leg on the table broke. Everything on it slid into the lady's lap—forks, knives, pepper, salt, four dishes, napkins, and the flower vase.

All the other customers were in shock either laughing or amazed. The owner of the restaurant came running to the table. The last thing I remember was her saying, "I'm so sorry! We will clean you up, and I will buy you two new dresses."

After everyone working there, including me, helped them to clean up, they then got up and left. That was the last we heard from them. They probably didn't eat dinner that night.

THE BIRD

When I was young I wanted a BB-gun.
A million times, I asked my father for a BB-gun.
At last, my father got a gun for me.

I saw a bird high on a tree.
I shot the bird.
The bird fell to the ground.

With gun in hand,
A long time,
I stood looking at the bird.

I saw a tree.
I saw the bird.
I broke my BB-gun against the tree.

Today, I am no longer young,

From that day until this,
My hand has never held a gun.

RIGOLETTO—TRAGIC COMEDY

D O YOU REFLECT on the many incidents that happen in life, as I do…some tragedies, others strange, and a few quite funny?

What I am about to tell you actually happened. Some of the details might not be accurate because more than sixty years have gone by, but the story will remain with me for the rest of my life.

I started to study the clarinet at the age of eight, and by fifteen I'd already had three different teachers. My plan for the future was to get into the Juilliard School of Music.

Finding places to play was a priority. Fortunately my father had a dance band, but when he could not use me, I searched for a classical group.

One day I was with a voice teacher, Madame La Pluma, at her apartment in New York City. She was always on the lookout for instrumentalists to accompany her singers as they rehearsed an opera. I had never had the opportunity to see and study opera music. I thought it was wonderful!

Most often at these rehearsals there was an unusual set of players. At times my clarinet might be accompanied by a violin, a trombone, a bass drum, and always with a piano.

Madame La Puma called me one day to ask if I would like to earn five dollars by playing a performance of the opera Rigoletto with some of her students singing. It would be my first payment for playing opera. I accepted the invitation with delight. It took place somewhere in New Jersey. I have no memory of the location.

Rigoletto is about a court jester who has a beloved daughter, Gilda. A duke falls in love with her. Rigoletto does not approve. It takes several acts to dramatize this situation.

In the final act, Rigoletto makes a deal with a gang to have the duke murdered. The dead body is to be put in a sack and brought to him. As he stands expectantly on the stage, four stagehands carry out a large and very heavy sack and place it at his feet.

Just before this climactic section, my clarinet broke down. Much to my consternation, I was unable to play. The orchestra, which sounded pretty awful anyway, didn't seem to miss me, so I relaxed and focused on the stage.

Once the sack is in front of Rigoletto, he expresses his happiness at the thought that the duke is dead by singing a joyful aria. Then, from afar, he hears another aria being sung. He is filled with trepidation, knowing that only the duke sings that aria. Bending down, he struggles to open the sack, and to his grief he sees that it is his daughter Gilda. She sings a couple of words—and dies. On this sad note, the opera ends.

The entire audience, including me, was laughing uproariously, though. Yes, laughing, not crying.

Why?

The giveaway dawned on us from the moment the huge sack arrived. It could not have been the duke, who was about five foot four and weighed maybe 130 pounds, but had to be Gilda, who was about the same height but must have been over 300 pounds. What an ending!

Then four stage hands reappeared and carried Gilda, in the sack, backstage. We were convinced that the opera would never be labeled a tragedy in our minds. The performance had filled us with glee. I was sure that anyone who was there that night would never forget it.

JOAN

WHEN I WAS A STUDENT at the Juilliard School of Music, I had many friends. Two of them were Vincent LaSelva and Joanne Amici. They have remained friends all these years.

Vincent started as a trumpet player and changed his major to conducting. He became, and still is, a top conductor in the opera world.

Joanne was a fine pianist but did not pursue a career even though she had lots of talent. We were good friends and honestly were not romantically involved.

When we graduated, I started my career, going on tours throughout the states playing the clarinet. Many times when I returned home to live with my parents, I got in touch with Joanne, and we spent time going to concerts and other musical events. She lived in an apartment at the Ansonia Hotel in Manhattan, and I would call her and meet her there when we had a date.

One day I was in her area and, without calling her, I went up to her apartment, rang the bell, and expected to see her. When the door opened, my life opened! There stood a beautiful blond. I thought that I had rung the wrong bell, but when I looked at the number on the door I was at the right place. It took me a few minutes to say, "Where is Joanne?" She answered, "She's not here, and I'm her new roommate, so please come in."

That was the end of her being a blond. She soon returned to her natural color, brunette. It was the beginning of my life with Joan, and marriage followed about one year later. It is now 2015 our fifty-fifth year together.

Her name was Joan Sena. Joan was, and still is, a great singer. Of course being her husband you might say, "He'd better say that." Well, just ask anyone—yes, anyone—who has heard her sing, and they will say the same thing. She has sung with the New York City Opera and at many other well-known places all over the world, and with Pavarotti and Domingo.

I am now going to finish this story by honestly saying that we have had our ups and downs, but many things have kept us together all these years: relatives, our wonderful two boys, granddaughters, many special friends, and our faith.

I'm sure that Joan feels just as I do. . .that is, one day we will leave this earth and get on an elevator that only goes up.

Metropolitan Opera

ROADS

ROADS OF LIFE: When we arrive on this planet, we really don't know where our lives are going to take us. Early on, a great deal depends on the path our parents have chosen. For example, if the family moves away from your birthplace, where you have already established friends, schools, and so on, it could be rather challenging, but often new and exciting avenues of opportunities appear.

I'm going to examine stations of my journey from early in my life until now.

They started when I was born. I don't remember much until I was in grammar school and a teacher named Mr. Marconi came to our school to teach clarinet. After a discussion with my father, who at that time made most of my decisions, we decided I should study with him. My father did give me one condition, which I still remember—that, if I were to start studying, I could not give it up unless he said okay. (He was paying a dollar a month to rent the clarinet and fifty cents a week for lessons.) My brother and my father were both clarinet players, and it seemed that I should follow this musical direction. It was the first big decision to influence the rest of my life.

The next important fork in the road came when I went to high school and took a music class with Ms. Mendelssohn. She played recordings of classical music that I had never heard before. One of them was a symphony by Brahms, the memory of which has remained with me all my life. I changed clarinet teachers while I was there, and some of the consequences were a bit rocky because I didn't feel that I was going in the right direction as a clarinet player.

However, toward the end of my high school years, I started to study with a man whom my father had heard of and who was the first clarinet player at the Metropolitan Opera, Gino Cioffi. He was really a terrific teacher. When I was senior, I was planning to audition for the Juilliard School of Music. However, Mr. Cioffi did not want me to go after graduation. He felt I was not ready and wanted me to study one more year and then take the audition. I agreed. I studied four, five, and sometimes more hours a day, took the audition a year later, and was accepted. This was like flying to the moon.

Juilliard was perfect for me. Not only did I play clarinet, but I also took all the music classes—including chorus (I kept my voice low) and theory classes, and played in an orchestra. The first year was wonderful.

However, I again felt that the clarinet teacher I had was not for me. Mr. Cioffi had left to become the first clarinetist for the Boston Symphony, and I was studying with a teacher who just wasn't helpful.

I finally went to see the president of the school and explained my problem. He gave me another teacher. This was another direction that changed my life. The new teacher, James Abato, started from the beginning, and in the next two years I really became a professional player. I still thank him for his influence.

Something else happened, too. After the third of four years at school, I auditioned for Tanglewood. (It is the summer music center in Massachusetts run by the Boston Symphony.) They play concerts all summer. Beside that, they run a student program that includes a symphony orchestra. (A small note: in those days, a student had not only to pass an audition to be accepted but also pay a fee. The practice of paying a fee ended years later.) I was accepted.

What an amazing summer! Getting some instructions from players of the Boston Symphony, getting to play in the student orchestra, and all my other musical studies were a wonderful growing experience.

After the summer, I went home and started to get ready for my last year at Juilliard, doing some free-lance work. In the music profession this means playing for different organizations without a steady job, playing with the Radio City Music Hall Orchestra and many opera companies. I was well on the way to somewhere...but where that would be I did not know.

Toward the end of that year at Juilliard, my last, I spoke to my father about going back to Tanglewood after graduation. He told me that the fee was somewhat high, and suggested that we could write and ask for a scholarship, so that he wouldn't have to pay the tuition. We did. In a short while, they replied that they would be glad to see me again, and that I would receive a scholarship. However, the letter also said that I would have to perform a duty while there. It listed a number of things I could do, such as usher at the concerts, become a bus boy, and such. At the bottom of the list, I saw the word librarian. I decided that this was something that would interest me, so I wrote back and told them.

Talk about forks in the road! Later on in life, this turned out to be the most important direction that I was to take.

When I got to Tanglewood, I was told to go to a building on the grounds and look for a Mr. Witicar. I found him; he said he'd been waiting for me. He told me what I was to do as his assistant librarian for the summer, for the rehearsals and concerts of the student orchestra. I was also going to be playing my clarinet. I was to show up at his office every morning (evenings for concerts), where he would have piles of music that I would bring to the rehearsal room or the concert hall. He had already organized the music; all I had to do was put it on the correct music stands, which he had told me how to do. Then, at the end of the rehearsal, I had to pick up the music and bring it back to the office. This was also my duty for concerts. It was as easy as pie.

One of the highlights of that summer was the student orchestra playing a concert conducted by Charles Munch, the conductor of the Boston Symphony. I played first clarinet, which had a couple of important solos. All went well, and I was truly flying high. As the summer drew to a close, I felt a bit sad and had no idea what the future was going to hold for me.

One day while still in Tanglewood, I was given another audition for a tour orchestra of the Boston Pops with Arthur Fiedler as conductor. I made it and was told it would start the following January, 1955. Summer ended, as did my stint at Tanglewood, and

I went home.

I started free-lance work once again. One of the places I was playing was with an opera company in Brooklyn. They were going to go on a tour of the States and asked if I would come. It was going to be in the fall of 1954, before the Pops tour, and I gleefully accepted.

That was my first full-time job, though it was only for about eight weeks. The tour with the Boston Pops in January was also about eight weeks. These tours were marvelous. . . traveling to many states and seeing things for the first time in my life.

When I got back home, still living with my parents in Queens, I again engaged in free-lance work. Then other jobs in New York kept coming—touring with a ballet company, a group doing Carmen Jones, an orchestra with the well-known conductor Montovani.

This all went on for many years. In 1959 I met Joan Sena, an opera singer, and we got married in 1960. We found a place in New York City, and I decided not to go on tour again. Somewhere around this time, I got a call to play as a substitute at the Metropolitan Opera. I played many times in the backstage bands that were part of different operas. One day I was asked to play in the pit with the complete orchestra. That was something! It was part of my free-lance work, but now that I was married I was really eager to get a steady job. I did try out for a couple of orchestras but either refused the jobs they offered or did not get accepted. This went on for a couple of years.

Then, one day, my whole life changed. I had just found a parking space on the street where we were living when a good friend of mine, Vincent LaSelva, walking up the street, saw me, and stopped to say hello. Just as he was leaving he said to me, "Did you know that there's an opening at the Met Opera for a librarian?"

I told him I didn't, and he left.

That night I thought about our talk, and the next morning I called the Met and asked for one of the music directors, George Schick. He was an excellent musician and one of the conductors of the orchestra. I had played for him a few times, and he seemed to like me. When I got him on the phone, I asked if I could come and speak to him. We made an appointment for the next day.

I went to his office and sat down. He asked me what was on my mind. After a couple of seconds, I said that I had heard that there was an opening in the library, and that I would be interested in the position.

He asked me a question I will never forget: "Have you had any experience as a librarian?"

All I could remember was the summer I spent in Tanglewood. "Yes," I said, "I was a librarian at the summer session at Tanglewood."

He said, "Okay, you got the job."

This is a true story. The reason I just wrote that is that it's never been, and I'm sure will never again be, that easy to get such a job.

It was 1963. I started the position in late August just a couple of months after Mickey, our first of two sons, was born.

Working at the old Met Opera, located on Thirty-eighth Street and Broadway, was most enjoyable. There was a Chief Librarian named Harry Schumer and another assistant, Eric Schaffer. Both of these men were a bit on the older side, and I guess that was a big reason why I'd received the position. When I first met them they told me what to do, which included preparing the music with all kinds of markings and putting the music on the proper music stands for both rehearsals and performances. I would come in around 9:00 a.m. each morning and I had many projects to do that Mr. Schumer had ready for me. When I had to work a performance at night, projects were set on my desk and I did them while the opera was being performed. Sometimes during the performances there were other things I had to do too, like setting up music for a stage band. (I would also play my clarinet in some of these stage bands and, of course, got paid extra for playing.) While I sat down and did whatever chores were put before me, it became a great learning period, and I really started to understand what being a librarian at the Met was all about.

Some of those chores were quite easy. The really difficult problems didn't come at the beginning. However, I had to really get involved, because the assistant, Eric, was going to retire and most important, Mr. Schumer was in bad health.

The really biggest challenge came at the end of my first season. For many years the Met went on tour of the States after the opera ended in late May. That spring they were going to France for the first time, and since Mr. Schumer was unable to travel, I joined them. It was wonderful—and the start of thirty-eight years in the Metropolitan Opera Music Library.

The very last performance at the old Met was a gigantic gala with many of the greatest opera singers of that period. As usual, it was a big job for the music library to prepare for that night. It went beautifully! The singers all sang to perfection, and all the music was played without a problem.

Then something unexpected happened. It's been forty-nine years, but for me it is as clear as yesterday.

The Saturday night gala ended around midnight. I was living in Queens and had driven my car into Manhattan and found a place to park on the street. When I got into my car about 12:30 a.m., I had to drive crosstown to get to the tunnel toward home. As I approached Sixth Avenue, I stopped at a red light. The light turned green, and I started to drive forward. As I crossed into the street ahead of me, a speeding car came from the avenue and cut me off. I slowed down a bit, and all of a sudden several police cars raced by me, chasing the car that had cut me off. I stopped and watched the chase go up the street. About halfway up, the speeding car crashed, and the police all stopped and got out to get the driver. I was stunned. In a few seconds, I was told to drive on. What a way to end my second season at the Met Opera. Two days later I went with the Met to Paris for two weeks to perform five different operas.

Two years later, in 1965, the Met moved to Lincoln Center to start another chapter of my life. Mr. Schumer left and soon passed away. He and I had gotten another assistant librarian, whom I had recommended. I was now in charge, and things were going quite well.

Dan Sagarman was the new person in the library. He was very much like I had been when I first started. I would give him projects and, even though he worked slowly, we kept things going. But I was really running the show, working with all the personnel above me: music directors, singers, the orchestra manager, all the pianists, and many others.

One of the conductors, James Levine, was named Music Director. There are many stories about him, but the most important thing I can say is that he is a genius, not only as a conductor, but in his knowledge of music, and his calm way of handling projects was inspiring. One day he came into the library and said that, since he was now the Music Director, he would like me to get brand-new parts for the orchestra when he was going to conduct his operas.

I said I would take care of it, though I felt that there might be a problem. I did not tell him, but most of the players marked their parts so that they could use their markings to play better. When I put out the new parts and Maestro Levine started to conduct, many members of the orchestra started to complain, "Where are our parts?"

As soon as the rehearsal was over, he called me and said, "Get rid of the new parts and give the players back the old ones." All went well after that. He hardly came into the library, except for information he needed. I really felt so secure at this time of my life.

Another fork in the road lay before me.

During this period of running the library, no one was actually known as the Chief Librarian. One day I was called up to one of the directors, who in a sense was my boss. He really didn't know then what was going on in the library. I was running one of the most important departments in the Met. All he seemed to know was that someone should be in charge called the Chief Librarian. He shocked me when he said that Dan Sagarman and I should share the position.

I left his office really upset, but something happened that again affected my life. I walked into the library and told Dan what had happened. He said, "John, no way can that happen. I know you've been running the office in the greatest way possible, and that position should be yours alone."

Another shock!

He immediately got on the phone and told the director that I should have the position, since I had been taking care of every problem and knew everything. He listened to the response for a short while, hung up, and told me, "John, you are now the Chief Librarian."

After my first two years at the old Met, Lincoln Center was a different world, and I stayed there for nearly four decades. Many of my stories about conductors, singers, and other experiences are memories that remain with me still, enriching my life and filling me with gratitude that my journey has been so successful.

METROPOLITAN OPERA SOFTBALL TEAM

WHEN I BEGAN WORKING at the Met, I was asked by one of the musicians if I could help him organize a softball team. The plan was that this team would play when the Met went on its spring tour.

We gathered musicians and chorus members together for the venture, and we got in touch with other orchestras and some groups in the cities we were going to visit and asked them if they had teams, and would they be interested in playing ours. We got some replies and discovered they were more than excited to play against us.

We were all full of anxiety, wondering if we would play well or be embarrassed on the next tour. When we finally started to play, we all realized that we were not a good team; however, we did win once in a while.

Besides the players, there were a few other Met people who came to watch us play. They were our cheerleaders. This went on for quite a few years, and we all enjoyed it a great deal.

Among those cheerleaders was a chorus member who was from Korea named Yu. He only spoke a bit of English. One game, we were losing, and as we were going off the field, Yu yelled out to a couple of the players, "I want to pray."

One of the players told him that we were losing so badly, prayers wouldn't help, but he could pray that we would do better in the next game. He continued to repeat his offer; we just looked at him, puzzled.

As we were just about to get on the field one day, he came to us and said, "When I was in Korea, I prayed third base."

After we all stopped laughing, we asked him to join the team. He fit in just right, playing as lousy as the rest of us. Now, whenever I pray, I think of Yu.

A NIGHT AT THE OPERA

IT WAS NOT REALLY A NIGHT AT THE OPERA, but everyone from the Metropolitan Opera assembled at Carnegie Hall for a benefit concert: orchestra, conductor, and singers. Also included in the wonderful evening were invited artists. One of them was Tony Bennett.

During one of the breaks at the rehearsal, I was milling around with the great baritone Robert Merrill and Tony. We were exchanging some stories and telling a few jokes. When my turn came, I told the following story:

A bunch of clams had died and were waiting at the gate to heaven to be permitted entrance. The gatekeeper (Saint Peter), said, "I have never had a problem with clams, so you may all enter, except on this card—there's something wrong, and I cannot permit a clam by the name of Sam to enter. Where are you, Sam?"

A little guy in the rear announced that he was Sam. He came forward and was told he had to go down there.

Sam turned around and started to go. As he was about to vanish from sight, he turned around to all the other clams and said, "I'm going to open a special café, and when you get permission, I want all of you to visit me down there."

Centuries later, these friends of Sam got together and asked the gatekeeper if they could visit Sam down there. They were given permission—with two conditions. One, they were to return no later than midnight; and second, they had to take their harps with them. You see, these clams were a part of Symphony Of The Air. So to return through the gates they had to show their harps. They all agreed.

A short while before midnight, they returned. As the gate-keeper checked each clam to see if they had their harps, one did not. When asked where it was, he announced, "I left my harp in Sam's Clam Disco."

Bob Merrill laughed.

Tony Bennett giggled and said, "I've heard that one already."

The break was over, and we all went on to finish the rehearsal. The concert was a great success. Though I have not had the pleasure to talk to Tony since then, I will never forget both the joke and short time together with both of them: You can't win them all.

A BEAUTY OF A STORY

I HAVE WRITTEN and will be continuing to write about my years at the Met.

When I first began working, I met a wonderful flute player, James, who became one of my best friends. He was a very shy guy.

When I went on my first tour, just after the season finished at Lincoln Center, James invited me to go to a special event in one of the cities where we were to perform. I did, and this was the beginning of something special that I got involved with for many, many years.

He took me to a place that took care of mentally challenged children. (He told me that he had a similar child.) We were joined by three other Met musicians. The idea was to play a short concert for these children. It was trilling to be there.

Being shy, James just got up in front of them and played some lovely music without any kind of introduction or explanation about the players or the music. He did a few of these events on that tour.

Sometime later, when we returned to New York, he said that he was having somewhat of a problem putting these events together and would like me to take over. I had, in the past, produced many concerts, especially to raise money for churches and organizations that needed funds, so I agreed.

Starting the next year and for many years thereafter, I put together concerts, not only for challenged children, but for seniors in residences. One of the things I did was to add to the number of orchestra members who came to play at the events. The concerts were always performed without any payment. The musicians got a return that was greater than any payment.

Besides the musicians, I asked three members of the Met chorus, who were my close friends, to sing at these concerts. The emotion was always high. Looking forward to them made all of us very excited. I was the conductor, and at one appearance I set up the orchestra, of about twenty musicians, on the stage and stood behind a small podium. To my left, as I faced the orchestra, with the children behind me, was a door for the singers to come and go as their song came up. Also to my left, at the end of the stage, were stairs leading down to where the children were seated.

The orchestra played the first selection. Then each of the singers came out and stood to my left and sang. Some waited at the door as I started the introduction of their song, then emerged.

The day I will never forget was the one on which Ann Florio was going to sing. She had a superb voice. I started the introduction and was only looking at the orchestra. As we got to where she was to start, I looked to my left and discovered to my chagrin that she was not there. Instead, I heard her voice and looked out toward the children—and there she was, singing to them. As she went up and down the aisles, children reached out to touch her, and she touched them. It was one of the most beautiful experiences I have ever had.

As she reached the end of her song, she came back to the stage and up the steps. I ran to her and gave her a kiss and a hug. I looked out at the children and their helpers and saw that many had tears in their eyes.

Ann passed away a couple of months ago, and after her funeral I met with many of her relatives and friends. Several people got up and told stories about her, and when my turn came, I told them this one.

Again, I saw many tears.

She was a truly a beautiful human being.

JAPAN

YEARS AGO the Met started trips to Japan. I have always felt that I was quite lucky to see so many cities in the States and many foreign countries. Small incidents remain with me, but one that I want to write down is as follows:

After a couple of times in Japan, the Met softball team made arrangements to play a Japanese team the next time we were going to return. To be honest, I can't remember any details of where we were going to play.

When we showed up at the field, all of us were shocked. There was a cheerleading group of about a hundred girls, and a band. The players on the Japanese team were dressed in uniforms that were better than those of any professional team that we had ever seen, and we were dressed as if we had come from the Bowery. They also had umpires who looked professional.

When we were ready to play, the Japanese team came to us and welcomed us with a bow, which was wonderful.

We lost the game, but who cared?

ONE OF THE WORST
DAYS OF MY LIFE

W HEN I STARTED to work as a Met librarian in 1963, I was told
that, every spring, after the season ended in New York, the
Met Opera went on a tour within the USA. They would perform
the same operas that were performed at the Met Opera, so as we
finished the tour operas at the Met, all departments would pack up
all the material, and it would be trucked to the first city where we
were going to perform. The cities, for the most part, were the same
ones to which we went each spring: Boston, Cleveland, Atlanta,
Minnesota, and some others once in a while.

My chore was to pack the music for each opera in separate
green boxes that were about three feet wide, two feet high, and two
feet deep. I would put the music in a box and mark it with a number—and, most important, I would put the name of the opera on
top of the box and cover it with heavy tape.

For many years the system worked really well. . .no problems,
and the operas were invariably a great success.

One year the head of the prop department, the one who handled all of the material that would be sent to the next city on the tour, asked me if there was a way to put music for two operas into one box, because there was so much material going into the trucks.

This had never been asked of me before; I said I would try my best and look to see if it was possible.

I found that I could do it. The truth now is that I cannot remember which two operas I put into one box, so let's say they were La Boheme and Carmen. The music for both was going to be performed in that order in whatever city we went to.

We were to perform La Boheme on a Monday night, Carmen the following night, and then, on Wednesday, the last day in Memphis, another opera, then leave the next morning for Dallas.

We reached Memphis Monday morning, and when I went to the opera house around 6:00 p.m., two hours before the performance was to start, I found my box and set out the music for the evening. All went well.

In all the years that I had worked at the Met, this system had worked flawlessly. I would get to the opera house early every evening, set out the music, wait until the performance ended, pick up the music, put it the box, and go back to my hotel.

The next morning, Tuesday, around 10:00 a.m., I went for some reason to the opera house. (I feel, in retrospect, that it was God who inspired me to go there.) I looked for my box of music for the Carmen and couldn't find it. Most workers who had set up the stage had already left. The only one left was the head prop person. I went to him and asked if he knew where the box was. He said he had no idea what had happened to it. My heart skipped a beat.

After another intense search, I was getting more upset. I went back to my hotel room and experienced one of the worst days of my life. I had no idea what to do. Without the music, the opera would not be performed.

At around 5:00 p.m., I went back to the opera house and crept over to where the music usually was. There before me sat the box with the Carmen music. Wow!

I found the prop guy and asked him how it had gotten there.

He told me he had called Dallas, spoken to either an official of the opera house or the truck driver, and told them that, the minute the truck arrived, they were to look for the green box, then get it to the airport and mail it back to Memphis immediately, and someone would pick it up.

That prop guy is my hero.

The performance went on as if nothing had happened. No one except God and the prop man knew about the turmoil!

Now you know, too.

HAUNTING MEMORIES

As I get older, it seems my memory is fading. I try to remember things that happened as I grew up, things about schools and so on. But here are two incidents that I have not forgotten.

When I went for my interview at the Met, it was with one of the music directors, George Schick. When he hired me, it was one of the greatest days of my life. I worked with him for many years and became very fond of him because of his musicianship and his personality. He also was a conductor, and the incident that I cannot forget happened one night during a performance of *Madam Butterfly*. He was conducting.

A step backward: Among our many chores as librarians, we had to set up all the music on the stands before both rehearsals and performances. In almost all of the operas, when we got the score, either from the library or from the conductor, we set it up on the podium. In my many years as a librarian, almost all scores were just one large volume. I would set it up and, at the end of the show, pick it up.

The score of *Madam Butterfly* came in three volumes. So that night I placed the Act I volume on the podium and put the other two scores on the floor of the podium. Typically, when Act I was over, I would put the second volume (Act II) on the podium.

I forgot! I was standing outside the door leading to the pit when Maestro Schick started to walk to the podium—and I almost fainted. I went into the dark area of the pit and looked. I saw him look down at the last page of Act I. The concert-master (a violinist) saw what was happening, quickly grabbed the Act II score, and gave it to Maestro. Act II started and all was well. What a relief!

The next morning I got call to come to Maestro's office, which I fully expected. He was profoundly gentle with me, merely told me to be alert in the future, and that he hoped that problem would not reoccur. It never did.

The second haunting memory, which happened on September 25, 1994, is cemented in my mind.

One day, while I was at my desk in the music library, a man came in and introduced himself. His name was Will Crutchfield, and he was an art column writer for the *New York Times* as well as a conductor (not at the Met). He had come to the library for some musical information, and I was most glad to help him. He came back a couple of times. On another day, he asked me if he could write an article about me and my work. I was thrilled and said, "Certainly!"

He returned several times and interviewed me. On September 24, 1994, the article appeared on half a page of the paper, which included a photo of me in the library. As I started to read it, I was thrilled. It described all my duties and gave a few details about my life.

I was truly in cloud nine. . .until I reached the last two paragraphs, which I will now quote:

> *And being known throughout the profession as a man who knows his business, he does a lively trade on the side. He handles the parts for the Opera Orchestra of New York, the annual Richard Tucker Gala, and other operatic concerts. He also takes care of Placido Domingo's orchestral concerts worldwide— including the Three Tenors extravaganzas. These are big-ticket, low rehearsal items, with multiple pieces and plenty of chances for foul-ups, so you need a librarian you can count on. And if you want the best, you have to pay. The three of them got a million-five each just for the warm-up concert in Monte Carlo, and then two million for the L.A. concert, before royalties. Mr. Grande says, "I see numbers like that, and I start thinking I want a piece of the action."*

The phrase "I start thinking I want a piece of the action" is one I don't remember saying, but I'm sure Mr. Crutchfield didn't make that up. Why did I say it?

It has haunted me since I read the article more than two decades ago.

ZIO PEPPINO

WE WENT TO PARIS with the Met as well to perform operas for about two weeks. Just the thought of going there was thrilling. When I told my father that we were going, he said that Zio Peppino, my uncle and the husband of one of my mother's sisters, would be in Paris when I got there.

He came from Italy and was a rather wild guy. I had gone to Italy with my parents in the late 1940s and met him. He had been wild then, and my father said, "That's the way he is." He said he'd write to him and let him know that I was coming.

When the Met got there, I had completely forgotten about Zio Peppino. I was busy doing my job, which kept me at the opera house from about 5:00 p.m. to the end of each show, somewhere between 11:30 and midnight.

One night, a few friends from the orchestra invited me to go to Les Halles after the opera, the wholesale market of Paris where fresh items were delivered—fruit, vegetables, and many other things—to be purchased by vendors the next day. Besides the trucks coming and going, there were bars and restaurants for people to have a great time.

We found a place and started, after midnight, eating and drinking.

We didn't get back to our hotel until 3:00 or 4:00 a.m. I hit the bed and was out in minutes.

At about 6:00 in the morning, there was loud knock on my door. I staggered over, opened it—and there was Zio Peppino. He hugged me and told me to get dressed, because he wanted to show me Paris.

What could I do? I got into my clothes, and off we went. Different places were very exciting to see, and we then got to the Eiffel Tower, he told me to get on the elevator and go to the top and see one of the greatest scenes in the world. I asked him to join me. He told me that he was afraid of heights, so I went up by myself. It *was* awesome.

However, I really started to feel tired. It was all wonderful, but I had to find a way to get a bit more sleep. When I got back down, Zio was waiting for me.

I wanted to tell him that I needed to get back to my hotel, but before I could get a word in, he told me that he was taking me to someone's house, Italians friends, for dinner, which was to start around 1:00 p.m. I couldn't refuse, so I went.

The dinner was delicious, and I had a splendid time. The minute it was over, I went to Zio and told him that I had to take a nap, which was what I did every day because the operas would keep me up late. So he took me back to my hotel.

This all had happened about three or fours days before we were supposed to be heading home.

I did not hear from Zio until the last day. While I was going into the opera house, he called out to me and said, "I have something for you."

He was carrying a large bag and told me to give what was inside it to all our family members when I got back to the states. I looked inside and saw six large salamis. What a way to end the trip! We hugged and said good-by.

As I was entering the opera house, a good friend of mine, a stage hand, asked me what I was carrying. I told him, "Salamis."

He said, "You'll never get past Customs at the airport with food like that."

I asked, "What can I do?"

He paused a minute and said, "Give me the bag, and I'll take care of it."

I did.

Getting back to the States, seeing all the people I'd missed, and dealing with so many others things, I completely forgot about that bag.

About two weeks later, the stagehand came into my office with it. He had put it in the sets of *The Barber Of Seville,* and when they arrived reclaimed it for me. I showed him my gratitude by giving him one of the salamis.

That was the last time I saw or had anything to do with Zio Peppino. He died a few years later—but when I made a visit to Italy a couple of years after that, Zio's stories went on and on. I'm sure God is still listening to him.

TRAIL OF THE
PLACIDO DOMINGO MUSIC

W HEN I WAS THE CHIEF MUSIC LIBRARIAN at the Met, I was naturally involved with all the music used by the opera and very much involved with most of the singers, and struck up a friendship with many of them. These artists would be in contact with me, not only about their needs at the opera but about personal needs, such as music for concerts that they were performing all over the world.

Concerts mean performing with an orchestra (or sometimes with a pianist)—not in a staged production, which an opera is.

One day Placido Domingo asked me to find some music for him that he needed for a concert he was doing out of town. I was most happy to do this. A few days later I approached him with a proposal. I told him to give me all of his personal music and I would take care of it. I would receive payment from the producer of his concerts when I sent all the music he needed. He would only re-imburse me when I purchased music or made transpositions for his collection. He agreed.

Taking care of music is a bit complicated. For example, when it is sent to an orchestra for a concert, I needed to make sure that all the parts were included and check again when the music was returned, to make sure all parts were there. I also erased all markings that were not important. I also had to have arrangements and transpositions made for artists who needed them. All of this music was cataloged, so that I could get whatever was needed immediately.

Besides Placido, I did the same for Renee Fleming, Sam Ramey, James Morris, Marilyn Horne, and Jennifer Larmore.

Now for the trail of the Placido Domingo music.

The story has its good and bad sides. The good side is that, when music was needed, I could easily take it out of one of the storage boxes and simply mail it out; after the performance, it was immediately returned. The bad side is complicated. One of Placido's problems was that he had so many commitments all over the world that getting information like a final program didn't happen until the last few days before a concert. This was okay when all I had to do was find the music that I had and mail it. But it often happened that I didn't have the music. Sometimes, I didn't get the exact mailing address either, or I had to fax copies to a singer who would be appearing with him. These problems had been going on for years. Luckily, I cannot remember any concert being either canceled or changed because the music wasn't there on time.

In December 2003, I was informed that there would be a concert in the Dominican Republic. I was to supply only about four selections, when I normally sent as many as twenty-five, and the rest of the program would consist of arrangements that would be new and made up for Placido and an accompanying singer. In the past, when he had new material made up, I got this material back after the concert and added it to his collection.

When the four selections that I had sent were returned, the new material that had been prepared for the Dominican concert was not included. I had no idea what it was or whether those selections would be needed in future concerts.

Early in February I was told that there would be two concerts in March, one in Germany and one in Russia. When I received the program list, I noticed that I did not have some selections that they needed, and found out what the new ones were that had been used in the Dominican Republic.

I got in touch with both Alvaro Domingo, Placido's son, and Nicki Marko, his assistant. Some of the selections were still in the Dominican, and some were in Placido's office in Manhattan. (One of the songs that I got from Alvaro turned out to be the wrong arrangement, which complicated matters even more. Alvaro confirmed this and got me the correct version.)

I also had to get in touch with Petra Weiss, another of Domingo's assistants, in Vienna, for a couple of other selections for the German and Russian concerts. (At this time I was looking for a space ship to get me away from all this incredible project of putting together music—no luck.)

I would estimate that over fifty emails traveled among Petra, Eugene Kohn (the conductor), Alvaro, Nicki, and me, attempting to get the correct music for these two concerts.

The events were set for March 6 in Germany and March 10 in

Russia. On February 24, I sent the music to both these countries. The package that went to Germany was delivered on February 27. The one sent to Russia, though, was held up in Customs for duties and fees. After another series of phone calls and emails both to Petra Weiss and Federal Express, the music was finally delivered to the orchestra on Tuesday, March 2, five days later.

All then seemed okay.

On March 4, two days before the concert in Germany, I received a phone call from Petra, who was in Germany during the rehearsal period before the concert. One of the selections that I had sent was the wrong version. The correct version was one that had been done for Placido in the Dominican Republic, which I had not received. After more phone calls, I found that this music was with Nicki Marco. I went to Domingo's apartment and, with Nicki, faxed ninety pages to Germany. We also sent by courier (a $450.00 expense) the same parts that we had faxed them.

It was still not over.

The next day Nicki received another call and was asked to fax another selection to Germany. Since I had worked with him sending the first selection on Thursday, which required reducing and marking that music, Nicki was able to take care of this last request without me.

And it was the *last* request, even though, after the concert in Germany, I was on edge thinking they might need something else in Russia for the March 10 concert.

But there were no more phone calls, emails, or other desperate messages.

I received an email after the Russian concert that read *Every-*

thing went well.

Music and payments were sent to me within two weeks.

I'm still looking for the space ship.

CONDUCTORS

Zubin Mehta

Zubin Mehta was a fine conductor. When he came to the Metropolitan Opera, he made a wonderful musical contribution to every performance. He conducted seven different operas from 1965 to 1971. All was invariably in order when he did so. He was really an excellent musician and, like some conductors, he memorized the entire score. This has its good and bad points. Conducting symphonic music with only the orchestra to worry about is a bit easier than conducting an opera, which requires paying attention, not only to the orchestra, but also to the singers on the stage. Conducting by memory gives the conductor complete control over the performance.

But one night at the opera, something unexpected happened.

The production of *Turandot* is one of the most difficult roles for any soprano, mainly because it is written with many high notes. High notes can be managed by most singers, but this role not only requires high notes but an ability to sing above the very loudly orchestrated accompaniment.

The great soprano Birgit Nilsson was to sing the role of Turandot. The rehearsals went just fine. But rehearsals are not performances. It's not like making a movie or taping a show. A performance at any opera house is live. Mistakes cannot be corrected until the next time around.

But the opening night of this opera, with the great Ms. Nilsson singing and Maestro Mehta in the pit, became something of a disaster. At one point, as Ms. Nilsson was singing, Maestro made a major mistake. He forgot a certain passage that took her out of the role. Exactly what happened is not clear. He might have conducted too slow or too fast. He might have forgotten to cue her in at the right time or had some lapse that caused a large section of the opera to fall apart. Orchestra, singers, and all involved fumbled for quite a while. Everything stopped for a few minutes, until Maestro called out a starting place. They rapidly responded, and in a very short while all recovered and went on to finish the opera.

This disturbed Ms. Nilsson enough that she went to Rudolf Bing, the general manager, and insisted that, if Maestro was to conduct this opera again with her, he must have a score on the podium in front of him. This was relayed to Mehta. A day of so before the next performance, I was summoned to bring a score to Maestro's apartment. When he answered the door and did not recognize me, he asked why I was there. I told him I had been told to bring him a score of *Turandot*. He laughed and took the score.

The night of the next performance, I went to his dressing room before the start of the opera to get the score, which was one of my duties, and put it on his podium. When I do so, I always open them to the first page, which I did that night.

As the Maestro entered the pit, I waited in a dark rear place of the pit to see what he would do. He climbed up to the podium and turned around to accept the usual applause from the audience. I was wondering what would happen next. He turned to the orchestra, ready to start, saw the score, and quietly closed it.

He conducted without looking at the music. It was a wonderful performance, and Ms. Nilsson was happy because all she had wanted was for the Maestro to have a score in front of him.

That was achieved.

Thomas Shippers

Shippers was a good-looking man. He was also very talented. The only thing most of us in the orchestra were not impressed with was that it seemed, at times, he was not well prepared. He would be conducting some operas for the first time and acting as if it was some kind of music from another planet. But he learned fast and, for the most part, was a favorite at the Metropolitan.

One incident remains with me because I was directly involved in a mess-up.

The Met was planning a Tchaikovsky opera, *Pique Dame*, which was to be conducted by Maestro Shippers. During the rehearsals a question came up by the leading baritone about an aria he was going to sing. He wanted to know whether the key was right for him.

Let me explain a bit about different keys, or transpositions. Almost every question about a transposition concerns a tenor or soprano—the notes of the aria in question go a bit too high for them to feel comfortable. So they need the orchestra music lowered a bit so that they will be able to sing without straining. It was our responsibility in the library to have transpositions available. Most of those transpositions had been used at the Met over many years, but once in a while a singer would request something that we didn't have, so it would have to be arranged.

The request by the baritone in *Pique Dame* was somewhat unusual, since he wanted the transposition to go *up,* not down: Some of the low notes were close to being out of his range. During the rehearsals, he tried both the original and the transposition but could not make up his mind what to sing for the opening performance. The plan was for Maestro Shippers to let me know the afternoon of the performance which would be used. He told me it would be the transposition. My system was to put a note, into each part of the music going in front of every musician, to use the transposition. Also, I put up a large sign outside the two entrances to the pit with the same information. So the musicians had both the original and the transposition, and were ready to play the transposition.

All seemed to be in order. When Maestro Shippers was making his entrance to start the opera, he again checked with me regarding the changes and seemed relaxed about it all.

Let me describe how a conductor communicates with the orchestra *during* a performance. There have been some performances when the use of transpositions are decided at the very last moment, so that notes and signs cannot be prepared. So the players are told as they walk into the pit, and hopefully everyone knows what to play. A couple of times, I had to crawl into the pit to notify players of a last-minute change. Conductors, knowing of such a change, will use a hand signal to indicate it. They point their thumb down, which tells the musicians to play the transposition. Remember, most transpositions are used by tenors or sopranos, so a thumb down means "play the transposition in the lower key." If the conductor is not totally sure the musicians know what key to play in and it is going to be the original, he will point his thumb up.

So when Maestro Shippers entered the pit, all seemed in order. When we got close to this part of the opera, I stood in the rear corner to listen for this transposition just a very short time before it was going to be sung—and looked up to see Maestro do something I will always remember. Instead of just conducting and leaving everything in place, he pointed his thumb *down*. But the transposition was supposed to go *up*, because that was what the baritone needed. If this sounds confusing, it also confused the orchestra players. Some played the transposition, and some played the original. When half the orchestra heard the original while they were playing the transposition, they switched to the original. The other half switched the other way. This aria, which went on for about four minutes, had never, ever been played that way. It was a total mess.

I was also a total mess. When Maestro came out of the pit, he came to me and said, "I should have kept my fingers to myself."

We never used that transposition again.

Karl Bohm

Sex at the opera happened at the Metropolitan in the 1970s. The opera was *Der Rosenkavalier*, by Richard Strauss, and this story concerns a ballet dancer and two dogs.

But first a word or two about the conductor, Maestro Karl Bohm. He was a staunch Austrian who had had some kind of connection with the Nazi regime. When he came to the Met after World War II, it caused something of a problem, but that passed and he became one of the main conductors in the '60s and '70s.

He was a very serious, dour man and, in those days, had all the people around him on edge. He didn't seem to know how to smile. One year I thought I pleased him by buying a new set of orchestral material for an opera he would be doing. I got this set in the spring, before the season, which was to start in September, so that I would have it ready for him when he came for his fall performances. When he arrived, I proudly announced that I had done so.

He blew his top and told me that the old material, which he had used for years and was now falling apart, had been marked by him years before, and that that was what he wanted to use. I lost a couple of inches in height and ten years of confidence. Later that day he came to the library and instructed me to get the new parts and insert into them every marking from the old parts. I did what he asked, which took me and my staff a few days. The performances went off quite well.

Maestro Bohm had a conducting style that was very difficult to follow, and new musicians in the orchestra were well warned of it. In those days some conductors conducted with what is described as a "hesitation beat." That is, when their hands came down to where the players normally are to play, the whole orchestra would play after hesitating a split second. This was done because conductors had to try and get both the players and singers to come exactly together. It didn't always work, and some performances were pretty sloppy. One day I was asked to play clarinet at the last minute in *Don Giovanni*, with Maestro conducting. Luckily the other clarinet player next to me, a veteran of the Met and the Maestro, told me not to play the first note. As I watched the Maestro come down for the first chord, I could thank my fellow clarinetist for his advice. If not for it, Mozart would have heard a version of *Don Giovanni* he had never heard before.

When Maestro James Levine came to the Met, he had a bit of a problem with this hesitation beat, but he trained the orchestra to play as most American orchestras do, which is to follow the beat. If you don't know what I'm talking about, go spend four years at Juilliard.

Now to sex at the opera.

Der Rosenkavalier is certainly one of Strauss's greatest and one of opera's most enjoyable. Maestro Bohm was the conductor.

The first act takes place in a large room in the home of the Marchilan, where, at one point, various service people come in: an Italian tenor, who sings a wonderful aria; the hat maker; the police inspector; the notary; and the animal trainer. In this production, the animal trainer character was played by one of the ballet dancers, and the costumes were of the period, which included large white wigs. When he came out, he had two poodles following him on leashes. He walked with his nose up in the air and he only had to parade slowly near the Marchilan.

Before he got to her, the dogs decided to have sex. It was a live performance. Since the trainer was standing with his nose up in the air and the dogs behind him, he had no idea what was going on.

But Maestro Bohm, naturally, saw it and started, as did many others in the audience, to laugh. I happened to be in the pit and witnessed it all. Seeing the Maestro laugh was like witnessing a miracle. The animal trainer finally left the stage, and the rest of the performance went on to a glorious ending.

Since that performance, two dogs have never again been used, just one, and most important, Maestro's attitude changed. Whenever I went into his room to pick up a score or for some other musical business, I would somehow bring up the subject of the Rosenkavalier dogs. He'd *always* laugh. The change was a delight.

Nello Santi

In my judgment, Santi was one of the greatest conductors the Met has ever had. He knew his scores like no one else. One day we had a vocal score (a book with the voice parts accompanied with a piano part, used for all rehearsals prior to the singers rehearsing with the orchestra), and three or four musicians were having difficulty finding a particular page of music. Maestro Santi took the book, which contained over two hundred pages, and turned right to the correct page.

He and I became really good friends, often going out to dinner with our wives and constantly being in touch when he was traveling. His home was in Zurich, and he conducted all over the world.

One day we made plans to go to a restaurant in Manhattan, a place he had been to many times. Our wives were with us. As we sat down, we all noticed that the tablecloth had bits of food on it. It looked rather dirty. When the waiter came to take our order, Maestro Santi said, pointing, "We will take one of these, two of these, and one of these."

The waiter almost fainted and called a couple of his co-workers to come to the table immediately and put on a clean tablecloth. We all laughed throughout the dinner.

One day in a conversation with him, I asked the date of his birthday; he told me September 23. I asked him what year he was born; he said 1931. I started to laugh and told him that I'd been born three days later. On another day he came into the library to get a score and, as he was leaving, turned to me and said, "Do you know that I have had three days more sex than you?"

We still keep in touch.

Fausto Cleva

One day on tour, as I was walking down a street with a couple of musicians, Maestro Cleva came toward us. We stopped to say hello and one of the musicians asked him, "Do you remember one of the greatest moments you had in your musical life?"

He answered, "I only remember the mistakes I and others made."

What an insight into genius!

James Levine

Maestro Levine made his debut at the Met in 1971 as a conductor and, in 1976, became the Musical Director. This title made him one of the top decision-makers at the Met. He was involved with the hiring of conductors, singers, musicians, and many other related musical personnel. As I write this about him, he still holds this position.

I had a relationship with him when he was first hired, but when he assumed the directorship, our time together increased. He would come to the library and talk to me about music material and many other subjects. I was called to his office many times to work with him. I am so proud that, to this day, we have gotten along so well.

One incident I will never forget was when he first became the Director. He came into the library and talked to me about the music for the operas he was going to conduct in the upcoming season. He said that he would like me to get a brand-new set of parts for the orchestra for each of the operas that he was going to be doing. I got them ready for the first rehearsal, which was the opera *Forza Del Destino*.

I went to the rehearsal room, as usual, just before the conductor came in. I looked around and saw all the players sit down and get their instruments out. Many of them soon looked disturbed. Maestro Levine came in and started conducting. A few of the musicians got up and complained about the new parts, saying that all the markings for themselves they had put into the old parts were not there. These markings helped them in ways too lengthy to explain.

After the rehearsal, Maestro Levine came into the library and told me to forget about the new parts and to put back the old parts. That was the end of that. For the next rehearsal I put the old parts on their stands, to the relief of them all.

Peter Magg

Magg was one the many guest conductors at the Met. He came to the library a few days before his first rehearsal, with the orchestra, of *La Traviata*. He wanted to look at the orchestra parts. I got the parts for him; after looking at them a few minutes, he called me over and asked if he could put all his markings into the parts. I told him that these markings had been put into the parts by the musicians and had been there for many, many years. (Some of our parts go back many decades, including a set of *Otello*, which was dated sometime in the 1890s). He was rather abrupt about it, telling me that he was the conductor and for me to do what he wanted. I said that I would speak to one of the heads of the music department. I did, and was told not to. I went back to him and told him so. I did suggest that he could buy a set of parts and I would make them with his markings for use if he was going to perform the opera in other places. He refused and went on to use our parts for his performances.

Carlos Kleiber

Almost every conductor that came to the Met was exceptional. They had different styles, but the end results, with the exception of just one or two, were splendid. I was a lucky guy to be working with so many of these conductors and, of course, many of the great singers. Maestro Kleiber, the son of another great conductor, and I got along very well.

One early morning I was making a pot of coffee for myself and the rest of the staff. Maestro came in to look for a piece of music. I asked him if he would he like a cup of coffee. He said he would be delighted. As he looked at the music he'd come in for, he enjoyed his cup of coffee with us.

A few days later, I received a note from Maestro that read:

> *Dear John! Sorry but I just didn't manage to get back to the theater. Thanks for everything! Hope to see you again soon! From CK.*

This note was inside an aluminum cup with another note:

> *A present for Mr. Grande of the library. If you please read the inscription on the tankard inside, you will see why I must leave it in NY! Please hold onto it for me.*

The outside of the cup read: *Carlos Kleiber, for use only at the Music Library of The Met Opera.*

Unfortunately, he never did return to the Met. I still have the cup.

Leonard Bernstein

In my eyes, Maestro Bernstein was one of the greatest musicians I ever met. His piano playing, his conducting, and his compositions were wonderful.

I have two little stories to tell about him.

I was in Tanglewood when the Boston Symphony was playing

George Gershwin's *Rhapsody in Blue* in the large covered outdoor shed, attended by an overflow audience. Maestro was playing the piano. This music has some very loud sections and a few very quiet parts played by the pianist. Maestro was playing and about halfway through the piece he had a beautiful part without the orchestra. The audience was captured and enjoying the moment. All of a sudden, a cymbal fell in the percussion section and made a sound that lasted a minute or so. Maestro stopped playing; the audience was stunned. When the sound stopped, he looked around both to the orchestra and the audience. Everything became quiet, and he started where he'd left off. I'll never forget that.

Maestro came to the Met and conducted a few operas. He dropped into the library a few times to check on a few musical things. I helped him as much as I could. One day he came to the library, looked at me, and said, "Good morning, Johnny." As long as he was at the Met, he always called me Johnny. How could anyone not remember this all their lives?

PRIMA DONNA

RIMA DONNA MEANS "first lady" in English. In the world of opera, a prima donna is sometimes a positive description of a singer and sometimes a negative one—negative because she sings wonderfully but acts like she owns the world, walks with her head high and talks like she is the best singer of all time.

In my first year at the Met I had a somewhat humorous incident, the memory of which has remained with me ever since. After a performance, I was in the elevator by myself. The door opened, and in came the wonderful soprano who had just finished singing. I had never had a chance to talk to her before, and I said, "You sang so beautifully tonight."

She looked at me and said, "And didn't I sing good last Saturday night?"

The elevator door opened again, and out she went.

What had I done wrong? Should I have said, "You sang beautifully tonight as you always do?" or "How do you feel after singing so beautifully?" or "What country do you come from?"

I have come up with so many questions I could have asked her. Maybe someday I will remember her name, and if she is in the place in which I hope to be, I will apologize for what I said.

WHAT DO I WRITE?

THERE ARE THINGS in my mind that must come out, but I have a problem finding them. They are hidden deep in the recesses. Last night in bed I came up with this story.

As you, who have come to know me, can see, many of these stories occurred while I was affiliated with the Metropolitan Opera.

Sometime in the 1980s, the Met made a trip to Tokyo to perform. We were going to be there for two weeks. As were most trips to other countries, this was truly a joy. When we had time, many of us took side trips to other cities in Japan and enjoyed everything about Tokyo: the food, the people, and all that makes up a great city.

When the Met goes to cities outside the States, the orchestra, the chorus, the stage hands, and many others participate. I would estimate that about 250 people came wherever we traveled.

Here is one of the most incredible coincidences I have ever encountered. It was spring, and the streets were packed every day as if it was New Year's Eve. Walking the city was a female chorus member who had brought along her husband. He had been a soldier in

World War II. They were doing some window shopping. As they were moseying along a crowded street, they began to look at something in a dress shop.

At that moment, a very respectable Japanese man said in broken English to the husband, "Excuse me—may I ask you a question?"

After a brief hesitation, the husband said, "Of course! What do you want to know?"

"Well, were you a soldier in the last war?"

"Yes, I was," answered the husband.

". . .Were you, by any chance, a guard monitoring captured Japanese soldiers on one of the islands the Americans had captured?"

"Yes, I was."

"Well, I recognized the back of your head and wanted to welcome you to Japan—I was one of your prisoners."

You can just imagine the man's amazement.

The story spread to all of us Met members, and now, forty years later, I'm writing it all down. I was told that the three of them then had lunch together. Then the Japanese man left.

Odds and Ends

JOHN

A FEW DAYS AGO, my wife Joan and I went shopping in the local supermarket. When we got to the fruit and vegetable section, she was looking for a package of basil, but couldn't find one. A young man was working there, and I asked him about it. He said that he would see if he could find a package in the back.

He returned in a couple of minutes and handed Joan the basil. As I thanked him, I noticed his name on a label on his shirt. "So your name is John," I said. "I'm also John. You know what? I don't meet any young boys with our name. It seems that, like John, names like Bill, Harry, Tony, Paul, and so many others aren't being used anymore."

He agreed; a few minutes later, Joan and I finished our shopping.

That night, when I was in bed, I remembered the incident and decided to write a story about the name John.

For clarity's sake, I will call the friends #1 and #2. No names until the end.

The year is 2114. Two friends meet after not seeing each other for quite a while.

#1: Hi! So glad to see you. I want to tell you that my wife is going to have a baby.

#2: Great news! Is all going well? Have you found out if it's going to be a boy or girl?

#1: Everything's fine. It's going to be a boy, and we're going to name him John.

#2: John? Who ever heard of that name?

#1: Well, my wife and I found a Bible, and when we started to read it, we saw many names that were used many, many years ago, so we decided to use one those. Names like Paul, Luke, James, and so many more. No one is using them these days. By the way, what's *your* name?

#2 Iyshobabxfro, and my last name is Io. People call me Io. What's yours?

#1: Misyxtmy, and my last name is Mozzarella. People call me Misy Mozz.

#2: Let's hope that someday we go back to John, Michael, and all those easy-to-say names.

#1: Well, we did make a start when we decided to name our boy John. By the way, a few weeks ago I got on the computer and tried to get info about my last name. I learned that, in the last twenty-five years, the computers have gotten over five billion things to look up, so if I want this info I'll have wait about one or two years. I'm waiting.

#2: Good luck. See you again, Misy Mozz.

#1: Hope to see you again, Io, and hopefully you will meet our son.

#2: Did you say his name is John?

BASEBALL AND MUSIC

'M A GUY WHO LOVES baseball and music. I wonder, when the time comes, whether I'll have a chance to meet Joe DiMaggio and Guiseppe Verdi, the two Joes.

I hear Verdi's music all the time, awake or sleeping. I see Joe hitting the ball and making great catches. I want so much to ask Verdi, "How did you write such incredible music?"

I sometimes pretend that I'm playing ball with Joe D. and conducting an opera by Verdi. I feel close to both J.'s when I see a baseball game or attend an opera.

I really want to be close to Joe and Guiseppe, but I worry that this will never happen.

Sometimes I cry when I hear music.

I understand much of my desire is just a dream. I say meeting with Joe or Guiseppe would make my existence complete. I dream of music. I try to understand where or when my life will end.

I hope, as I have said for years and years, that I will meet them. I'm a guy who loves baseball and music.

GARAGE SALE, 2008

A S MANY MARRIED couples know, most times they think differently. I am not going to list the differences between my wife and me. That would take volumes. Instead, I am going to describe how we agreed to have a garage sale.

People who have been married close to fifty years accumulate an incredible amount of what I call junk and my wife calls treasured items.

We started to gather items for this sale two years ago, and finally, with the help of one niece and two grandchildren who carried and priced most of the items, we picked a Saturday and Sunday in June to have the sale.

I put ads in the local newspapers, and early that Saturday we moved all the items from the garage to the driveway. (Since one of the ads had come out early in the week, I did get a fellow who came on Thursday, saying that he was leaving town and could he look at the collection. I said sure, and in about five minutes he took a few things and gave me $13.00. Good start!)

Saturday morning we intended to start at 9:00 a.m. People started to come around 8:00. About a hundred and fifty came. I would say that over a hundred of them walked up and down the driveway without stopping and, of course, not buying any items. Most people who were interested in some things felt they would be cheated if they didn't negotiate. Since I really wanted to get rid of all these things, I was negotiating the entire day. One guy found an item with a price of fifty cents. He talked to me for about five minutes, and I let him have it for twenty-five cents.

Around noon I got pizza for my helpers.

As the day wound down to the 5:00 p.m. closing time, and because the weather forecast for the next day was for rain, we decided to put all leftover items in the garage.

The next day, Sunday, was, as expected, a rainy day and about six people showed up. There were many items left.

On Monday I called the Vietnam Vets, and a few days later they picked up everything. We were free of our treasure-junk.

Here is a financial breakdown of the garage sale:

Expenditures	Earnings	Profit
Ads $40	$70	$15
Pizza $15		
Total $55		

Time spent, 16 hours—so I earned less than a dollar an hour, and four people worked. I'll never have a garage sale again!

A BUMPY ROAD—A FANTASY

PETE AND PHYLLIS were sweethearts in their late teens and got married in their early twenties. They tried to have children but couldn't. However, they were very happy. They both had jobs, and money was no problem. They purchased their own home when they reached the age of twenty-five.

The house had two floors with the bedrooms on the top floor. All was well for a few years until, one night, Phyllis heard Pete snoring, and Pete heard Phyllis snoring. When both of them snored at the same time, it sounded like a symphony orchestra with two solo tubas.

All was well so long as both of them were sleeping, but when one heard the other it became a nightmare.

One day, after a horrible night, they were having breakfast and talked about the night with the orchestra in the room. They decided that one of them, Phyllis, would move to the room at the end of the hallway.

Their sex life was very normal. When first married, they got it on many times a week, then, also normal, less than many times a week. When Phyllis moved to the bedroom down the hallway, it stopped for a short while, but they both enjoyed wonderful sleep time.

One night Pete, while watching the TV, rose to get a drink for both them. As he gave her one of them, he touched her hand, then ran his fingers up her arm, and on from there.

Phyllis said to him, "I'm going up to my bedroom and I wish that you would visit me."

Pete answered, "Of course I'll be there."

After he finished his drink he went up to his room, took a quick shower, put on his best-looking pajamas, turned off his lights, and started down the dark hallway. It was his first trip to Phyllis's room at night. Just as he got to the door, he banged his head on the wall. By the most incredible timing, Phyllis had gotten up to go to the bathroom in her bedroom and did not hear this collision.

Pete fell to the floor, somewhat dizzy. His head was bleeding, and he slowly got up and headed back to his room, where he started to clean up his head. He was not feeling well, fell into his bed, and fell asleep. A bumpy road.

Phyllis had been anxiously waiting for him in her bed. After a while she really got tired and, before she knew it, fell asleep.

The next morning at breakfast, Pete told her what had happened, and she, seeing his head bandaged, realized why he hadn't shown up.

When Pete left for work, he stopped at the local hardware store and bought a flashlight.

GIVE US THIS DAY OUR DAILY BREAD—A FICTION

VANCE AND ZILDA were married during the Depression, when times were tough. At first they struggled; then Vance started a bread-baking business, and things improved. They had two children, John and Mary. All seemed to be going OK except for one problem.

Every morning when Vance came down for breakfast before going to work, either he or Zilda would start small arguments. Vance might say, "The toast was a bit burned."

Zilda would grumble, "It's the same as yesterday."

She might say, "Must you always wear that shirt?"

And so the small argument would start. He would finish breakfast and leave for work feeling a bit down.

This happened almost every morning except for Saturdays and Sundays. Saturday Zilda would get up, clean the house, and go shopping.

Vance would sleep late and get up to a quite house, except when the children, who were really wonderful children, would make a little noise.

Then, on Sunday, the whole family would go to church, even though it did not seem to have an effect on Vance or Zilda. It was sort of taken for granted: They would say the prayers, listen to the sermon, and leave. It was very routine.

Once in a while Zilda would bring up the subject of God.

Vance would immediately say something like, "Isn't going to mass every Sunday enough?" That was the end of the subject.

The bread business grew more and more successful. Vance was finding ways to make different-tasting breads, and his customers were literally eating them up.

One day he started to make a bread that was completely different from any he made before. He worked on it for weeks. For some reason that he could not explain, every once in a while during this new bread making, he would stop and say a brief prayer, asking God for help.

With his concentration on this project, the morning arguments seemed to be stopping. As he went to work, things were not the same. He was changing. Zilda noticed this change and started to improve herself. So life was more peaceful.

Sunday came and, as usual, the family went to mass. Everything became clear as they repeated one important sentence. During the Our Father, the words "Give us this day our daily bread" made both Vance and Zilda stop and look at each other. When mass was over, the family stayed in church by themselves for a short while. They then got into their car. It was silent.

Vance finally said, "Family, today for the first time in my life I heard God. When we said, 'Give us this day our daily bread,' I not only thought of bread but of every other thing in our life that is precious, such as health, friendship, and especially love."

Zilda took Vance's hand and held onto it.

When they got home, she said that she had prepared a wonderful feast. In a few minutes, they were all seated and ready for this meal. As their son reached for a dish, she said, "Please wait a moment. I want to start each meal from now on with a prayer."

Vance said, "That's a great idea, but before the prayer give me a couple of seconds to get something from the kitchen." He left the table, returned with a large loaf of bread, and said, "This is my new bread, which we will now eat, not only as food, but to always remind us of the line, 'Give us this day our daily bread.'"

A miracle of God's love had begun to transform their lives.

INSTRUCTIONS

BEING AT THE AGE that many of you are who may be reading this, I want to write and talk all about a certain subject that has been on my mind for many years. And that is about how many divorces now take place in our world.

Let's start with many young people turning about seventeen or so years old. I remember this time and have seen and read about all the years up to now.

When a couple meets, what really attracts them mostly is their looks. Of course, the next step is conversation that gives each only a bit of what the person is all about. If this relationship goes further and gets more personal, then the next step, in many cases, is sex.

Before I go on, I will jump way ahead to married people. Yes, sex is great, but after a while it is not what keeps people together.

And now I really get to my point. If youngsters would spend more time with a list, either mental, or written out, I really believe that many of the problems that happen after marriage would be somewhat solved or at least discussed, and sometimes that will stop a marriage, and both will go on from there. Here is what I'm talking about. Let's say the girl is rather sloppy about her room and her house, and the guy is neat. They never talk about it, and if they do, she will say, "Don't worry. If we get married, I'll take care of our house." If this doesn't happen, it may become a major problem for both of them. Add to this list how to handle money, how to raise children, where to live, what kind of car to buy, sometimes the food they eat (he likes Chinese food, and she likes only Italian food), the list goes on and on. I'm not really saying that this will break up a marriage; however, in many cases it does.

So to conclude, what do we do? Of course a lot of this should be handled by parents and they should think about the way to instruct their children. Is this happening? I don't think so. What do you think?

CLOUDS—A FANTASY

I WASN'T FEELING very well one night. I said my prayers and before I knew it I was asleep. In a short time I awakened in clouds. Immediately I knew what had happened. I had died.

There were millions and maybe more people around. I jumped for joy when I saw my father, mother and everyone who had passed away. WOW? This was great. Hugging, kissing and crying, I asked my father what was going on in these clouds. He told me that most of the people I was looking at had already passed the test to get them past the gates of heaven, and that he and many of the others were there to greet the ones that were just arriving. I asked him, "How do I get in?" He told me that I would have a quick talk with Saint Peter or one of his assistants who had all my earthly records. "Sometimes many people go right through the gates," he said. "However, many people might have a problem, for example, if a person had no reason to kill someone, that person must fill out an application and go to a private meeting with one of Saint Peter's assistants. See that man walking over there. He has the applications.

So, the first step is to go to that gate and ask if you can just go in. If not, go get an application. Got it?"

"OK!" I started to walk to the pearly gates past millions of people. I did not recognize most of them and got on line. Right in front of me was a really elderly woman. She looked so sad and I asked her, "Are you alright?" She looked at me and said, "Who are you and why are you asking me how I feel?" I was a bit shocked by her answer, especially where we were. I said, "I'm sorry if I hurt you but you look so very sad and I wondered why." She said, "None of your business!"

We were moving very slowly. She then turned to me and said, "I'm sorry" "That's OK," I replied. She said, "I'm really nervous about this interview coming up." I told her not to worry. From what I had always heard from many of my friends, Saint Peter will forgive almost everyone if they can explain why they lived the way they did. "Do you understand what I just said?" She answered, "I guess I do, however I was a miserable person down there."

"By the way, may I ask you your name?" She said, "Ann." "Ann who?" I asked. She answered, "Ann Finley Sweeney." I almost fainted. "Do you mean, Ann Finley Sweeny from Ireland?" "Yes."

In my life I have met many people whom I have liked very much, and one of them was Jean Sweeney. We spent once a week at a writing class and she wrote some very personal stories about her family. She wrote these stories so that her children would be able to read them when she came up to these clouds. A couple of these stories were about Ann Finley Sweeney, her mother-in law. According to Jean, Ann had some crazy ways and didn't seem to like her. Every time she was with her, it was close to a nightmare. However, she found ways to get by.

As the line got a bit closer to the application desk, I decided that I wanted to know why Ann was the way she was "down there." I asked her, "Ann, why were you the way you were 'down there?'"

She answered me, "You do have questions after questions, why?"

I said, "I don't really know except that I have always felt something about sad people."

"OK," she said. "I was brought up in a long line of families that always made the women in the household the boss of everyone that lived with them. When I was born, my mother, her mother (and back and back with all the mothers) were the control people in the families. We had to make sure we married men that we could control. If not, it would be a terrible time for all."

Ann had had four children. . .two boys and two girls.

She had four rules.

When the four children got ready to get married they had to make sure that the women the boys married and the two girls were the boss.

If it didn't work out at the beginning of their marriage, they should find a way to break up.

When children came, again the women should teach them from the very beginning these rules.

And finally, all should prepare to teach the children by having a couple of straps ready to use when the children did not follow the rules. The first strap should be used for children around the age of four. This strap should be very thin and wouldn't hurt much. The next strap should be heavier, for the next stage of their lives and so on.

"So, when my son Paul met Jean, I was hoping that she would follow the family ways. No way! First of all, she and Paul got along just fine, against everything I wanted them to be. They seemed to both be in complete control of each other and the many children to come. So, every time we were together I couldn't get used to this change, and I guess I didn't get along with her. (By the way I had a talk with my son and asked him if he would leave her. He told me to go to hell.)"

I was amazed with what she told me as we got very close to the desk. She was then called up and in a short time left the desk and walked into more clouds.

I was called next and in a few moments also left and went into the clouds.

Soon I saw Ann and ran after her. I asked her what had happened. She looked at me for a while and finally said, "OK! You want to know what they said and I will now tell you. They gave me a bible and told me that I had one hundred years to read it, then come back to the table and we would talk again. I guess I don't have any choice."

She then started to walk away. I called out to her and said, "Ann, you dropped something." She bent down, picked up a strap and disappeared.

SPEEDING—2004

I RECENTLY GOT A TICKET for speeding. I was doing eighty miles an hour in a fifty-five-mile-an-hour zone. I went to court and, after spending a few minutes with the prosecutor and judge, I was given points and had to pay a fine of $430.00.

Before I explain why I was going that speed and got that ticket, I have to admit that I am a left-lane driver and, where I live, that means "driving with the tide." Traffic is usually heavy enough that everybody in the left lane is going about the same speed. This speed can easily be from five to fifteen miles higher than the posted speed limit, depending on the number of cars. I have been doing this for as long as I can remember, and I'd never received a speeding ticket.

This one night I was traveling north on the New Jersey Turn-pike and approaching the Meadowlands toll booth. There were only two lanes and, as usual, I was in the left lane. The right lane was full of trucks. I was keeping up with the trucks and knew that the toll plaza was only a mile or two up the road. I then saw a couple of signs that read *Left Lane Closed*. I couldn't get in the right lane because of trucks, so I sped up, finally found an opening in the right lane, and slipped between two trucks. I followed the truck in front of me, went through the toll plaza, and continued to follow the truck.

A police car came up behind me a mile or so later and pulled me over. I was given a ticket. I tried to explain what had taken place, to no avail. I guess I deserved the ticket, so after paying the fine, I thought that I would do something that would be new to me.

No more left lanes. So here's what has happened.

I discovered staying in the right lanes and doing the speed limit is dangerous. *Everyone* speeds. If you keep the speed limit, tailgating becomes another problem. Try doing thirty-five, forty, or fifty miles an hour when posted, and you will see what I mean.

I tried to drive another way. I was on the West Side Drive, again in the right lane and keeping the posted limit of forty miles per hour. With the exception of one other car, driven by an elderly gentleman, *every* car passed me. On the Garden State Parkway or the New Jersey Turnpike, where I received my ticket, speeding is a way of life; I just wonder how many have received tickets.

I have a possible ploy.

Property taxes! They are high and it seems everyone is looking for a way to lower them. Well, if one policeman gave out ten tickets a day, that would add up to about four thousand dollars. Multiply that by a hundred policemen giving out tickets every day, and goodbye property taxes.

On second thought, it would never happen.

One last insight. A way *not* to get to your dentist's appointment that you don't mind missing is to do the following: Get in the right lane. Go the listed speed limit, and keep the legal distance between you and the car in front of you, one car length per ten miles. If you are going, say, fifty miles an hour, you should have five car lengths between you and the car in front of you; but if you try to maintain this distance, many, many cars will slide in between you and that car in front, so you have to slow down to keep this distance. Eureka! You will never get to the dentist in time.

THINGS ON MY DESK

Hᴇʀᴇ ᴀʀᴇ ᴀ ᴄᴏᴜᴘʟᴇ of lines from phrases I have put on my desk:

Want to pick on somebody, get a harp.

I've always been crazy, but it keeps me from going insane.

Have you left the one you left me for?

I'm having day dreams about night dreams in the middle of the afternoon thinking of you.

Why don't you go home? Your clock needs re-winding.

If I say, "You have a beautiful body," would you hold it against me?

This is a sign in a local fruit store: *Do not put the nuts back after eating them! You are on film.*

This was sent to a newspaper:

> *Dear Diary,*
> *My husband and I took our three children to*
> *the Children's Zoo at the Central Park Wildlife*

Center.

We were happily giving pellets to the goats when I noticed a little boy (equally happy) shoving the pellets into his month.

Before I could warn him that he could make himself sick, his mother grabbed his hand out of his mouth, and upbraided him with the following words: "Don't eat those, silly, they're not kosher."

SOMETHING OF A SHORT STORY

MARY LOOKED INTO THE MIRROR and decided to put on her best-looking earrings and necklace. She was going to try and have a special evening going to her best friend Lucy's birthday party.

She always dressed fabulously, especially for these eventful evenings. She stood up, looked around the room, and for a moment was sad but soon smiled, called her maid, and told her to call a taxi.

In fifteen minutes she was in the taxi and about half hour later pulled up in front of Lucy's house. She got out of the taxi and walked up to the front door. At the same time a gentleman arrived at the door. He gave her a look and a quick nod and said, "Good evening."

She said, "Same to you, sir."

The door opened, and Lucy hugged Mary and excitedly said, "So glad you came tonight." She then said to the man, "Hi, Charlie, great you're also here."

They walked into a party room with many guests already there. More were arriving, and the home was full of excitement. There was a bar set up and a table with plenty to eat.

Mary loved to have a drink or two, but not much more. She always wanted to feel in control.

After Lucy went to greet other guests, Mary went to the bar and got herself a drink. She found a small table and sat down. She took a sip and looked around for some folks she might know. As she picked up her glass for her next sip, someone quietly said to her, "Mind if I join you?"

She looked up, and it was the man she had met at the door. "No problem. Please have a seat," she replied.

"I'm Charlie, a close friend of Lucy's husband."

"I'm Mary, close friend of Lucy."

"I'm a bit surprised we haven't met before," he said. "You a friend of Lucy and me a friend of her husband, I mean."

"I guess you don't eat lunch with Lucy. That's where I spend most of my time with her."

"Anyway, hello again."

"Hello to you! Is your wife here, or don't you have one?"

He replied, "I did. . .she passed away three years ago."

"Sorry!"

"What about you," Charlie asked. "Married?"

"My husband also passed away. It will soon be five years."

". . .You know, we've been talking for a few minutes, and I've really forgotten until now to tell you how beautiful you are. Your dress is absolutely lovely, and your jewelry and earrings and bracelets are special."

"Thank you! You look great, too."

"I'm sure your husband treated you quite well. What did he

do?"

There was a long pause before she said, "Would you please get me another drink? I don't think I can answer your question without a couple more sips."

He got up and, a minute later, returned with the drink. "Well?"

"Well what?"

"I asked you what your husband did before he passed away."

"Oh, yes. Okay, I'll tell you, but please kept it quiet. He was a bank robber."

Charlie didn't know what to say, and the ensuing silence stretched out. "You're kidding," he finally managed. "Go on and tell me what he really did for a living."

"Want to hear more?"

"Sure!"

"Well, I met Paul twenty-five years ago, and we immediately fell in love. He always treated me like a queen. Whatever I wanted, I got. As we courted, it was quite a life. Finally, one day he asked me to marry him. It was a tough day. For a long time, I had never asked what he did for a living...but when he brought up the subject of marriage, I finally said to him, 'Don't you think that you should tell me a little about yourself, especially what kind of work you do?'"

"'Well,' he said, 'when I answer that question, one of two things might happen. You might faint and leave me, and I'll never see you again, or, after you faint, you'll ask me a couple of hundred questions, then marry me.'

"'Okay,' I told him, 'let's stop fooling around. What in the world do you do?'

"'...I rob banks.'

"I tell you, I fainted dead away. He helped revive me. 'You're kidding me, of course,' I finally said.

"'No, I'm not.'

"'…I'm not leaving you just yet,' I said, 'but let me ask you a couple of questions. First, when did this robbing banks start?'

"'In my mid-twenties.'

"'You…you've been robbing banks for twenty-five *years?'*

"'Let me explain a few things. I was born, along with my two brothers, to parents who were, to say the least, extremely intelligent. My brothers and I seem to have inherited this trait. All three of us did extremely well in school, and we all went to college. I was the oldest and decided to study engineering. My next brother, Phil, studied accounting, and the youngest brother, John, really didn't have much of an interest in any special subject, so he went to a cooking school. We all graduated and were doing fairly well…. One day we were together, having dinner at a place where my brother John was the cook. He came out of the kitchen and sat down with Phil and me. The conversation was what it usually was: sports, girls, and money. There had been something on my mind for a long time, and I felt then was the time to tell my brothers. I started by asking both of them how they were doing financially. Both said only fair. "Well," I said, "I have an idea to make lots of money." Both of them leaned closer to me, and I said, "How about if we rob banks?" It took a while for both of them to stop laughing, but when they looked at me they finally realized that I was serious.

"'Phil then asked, "What are you talking about?"

"'John said, "This is like a bolt from the sky."

"'I said to them, "Let me explain. I have finished engineering school. I have spent a lot of time thinking about this new project and putting all the hundreds of pieces together: places where banks might be easier to rob, and all the details, and I firmly believe that I have come up with an unbelievable way to be successful.

"'"I would need two other pieces for this to work. One would be what to do with the money we earn, and the other to help me in doing this job. So John would be my helper, and you, Phil, would find out how to handle the money.

"'"What are our chances? Well, I have spent, and will continue to spend, enormous time going over every detail. I will explain every detail to you both and we will go from there. I really feel we would never get caught.'"

Ann said, "And that's the story. So I accepted this proposal, and we got married and lived a wonderful life until he passed. Any other questions?"

"So," Charlie said, "your husband robbed banks for over forty-five years and never got caught. He died a couple of years ago and left you and his two brothers with millions. It seems your brother-in-law, Phil, knew how to invest and hide, and live a very comfortable life, along with his brother John and, of course, you. I'm impressed."

"Now that you know what kind of life I've had, I have to know what you do for a living."

"You sure you want to?"

"Let's not go through that again. Of *course* I want to know."

"But no fainting allowed."

"Go ahead."

"I'm an FBI agent."

WHERE ARE WE GOING?

MANY OF US WHO BELIEVE in God have our own vision of where we are going when we pass away. Many of us feel that we will meet Him, and that He will show us all about what eternity will be like.

Also, we hope for things like meeting our father, mother, and all those who had been in our lives. I hope so. Also many of us have their own things they wish for.

Here are mine.

I want to spend time with people like Puccini, Verdi, Beethoven, and other composers. Also, some jazz musicians. One of my favorites has, for all of my life, been Artie Shaw. Since I also played the clarinet, he always knocked me out with his great talent for improvising. Here is one of the questions I would want to ask him. When he recorded "Begin The Beguine" and started his solo, I wonder if he made it up during the recording session, or did he have it all written out before the session. This will be a question for most of the great jazz musicians who made many recordings.

Puccini.

I have a feeling that when he was on Earth he did have a meeting with God, who gave him ideas for writing operas. How else can someone do what he did? Also, all the others who wrote seemed to have gotten messages from heaven. Verdi, Beethoven, Bach, and on and on. I tried writing music at one time but never got a visit.

What about people like Hitler? What was on his mind to do what he did? What hate he had. Why? I feel that I will not be able to talk to him, unless I can take an elevator down there.

When my parents passed away, they did not leave me with enough information about their lives. Again, I would like to talk with them and all my other relatives. What a party we will have. I pray that God and all saints will join us.

So I leave this short piece in the hope that the things I just wrote about will come true. I will pray for that.

MY WIFE'S QUESTION—A FICTION

MY WIFE ALWAYS ASKS me the same question: "Why do you spend so much time watching sports events on TV?" I have finally found the real answer. It came to me in a dream.

One night, watching a baseball game that had just ended, I died.

I found myself on a long line with millions of people headed to the gates of heaven. We were all moving very slowly. I took a glance backwards and saw a person who looked like Saint Peter. He was stopping every few feet and talking to people on the line. As he came closer to me, I noticed that he was asking a question that no one seemed to know the answer to. When he was in speaking distance, he asked, "Our Lord was so busy last night, he didn't have the time to watch the game between the Yankees and the Red Sox. Anybody see the game?"

I raised my hand and said, "I did."

"Oh, good. What was the final score?"

"The Yanks won 4-0."

He took my hand and led me to the front of the line.
My wife's question was finally answered.

STOP THE NOISE

BEFORE RETIRING, I used to get up at 7:00 a.m. to go to work. Now, one of my joys is getting up whenever. Most of the time, it works. But a number of times a week, it doesn't.

First, the garbage truck that comes twice a week and reaches my street between 6:30 and 7:00 a.m. Besides the sound of the truck, which I can hear from about a block away, there's the noise of squeaking brakes. Isn't there a law against squeaking brakes? I once called the company that sends this dreadful noise-making machine. They fixed the brakes, but that only lasted a couple of days. They probably sent another truck.

Second, there are people cutting their lawns. I envision a guy with a watch, standing under my window, and exactly at 7:00 a.m., when it becomes legal to make as much noise as you wish, he points to three other guys, and they start their machines. This seems to always disturb my dreams about a peaceful island, where the only noise I hear are waves gently coming ashore.

Third are the trucks that pick up snow and leaves. Why does it seem that my street is always their first stop? Can't they start somewhere near the Pennsylvania border? These trucks not only are loud, but emit a horrible beeping noise when they move in Reverse. Can't they at least have a tune put in so that, instead of ear-splitting beep, I could hear something like "Oh, What A Beautiful Morning"?

I'm thinking of going back to work.

ON AND ON

MOST OF US HAVE PEOPLE we know who have habits that could easily annoy us. For the most part, especially if they are good friends or relatives, we can live with their quirks, and they with ours. Most of us would probably agree that one of these habits is talking too long on almost any subject. Some do go over the top in expressing themselves.

Many years ago, I was introduced to a man who could easily have won an award for being the most unrepentant talker of all time. His subject didn't matter, or how he started. Once he had the floor, watch out.

This is an example of what I'm referring to.

I ran into Joe in the street and said, "Hello, Joe, how are you today?"

He answered, "I feel just great, nowhere like how I felt yesterday. Yesterday I had an appointment with my doctor. I really wondered if I should go. Only a week ago, on my way to see this doctor, I ran into an old friend of mine. He was on his way to get an early morning cup of coffee and asked if I'd like to join him. I said, 'Let's go.' On the way to the coffee shop, I stopped in front of a shoe store and looked at all the samples in the window, and I took my friend inside to have him help me find a pair of shoes that would look good on me. The salesman took out about ten pairs of shoes, none of which I liked. So we left. Walking down the street, I asked my friend if he was still married. He said, 'No,' and he told me had gotten a divorce about two years earlier. I told him that I knew another friend who *also* got a divorce, about eight years ago, and that he almost killed himself because he was so depressed. I had another friend that *did* kill himself, not because of a divorce, but he had no money left after gambling …" and on and on and on.

This conversation went on so long that he missed his appointment with the doctor. I'm sure the doctor was not too sad about that.

TO THE MANAGER OF STARBUCKS

Dear Sir,

Here is a story related to the enclosed book.

An elderly couple came in front of a judge who said to the woman, "You were caught on camera stealing in the local supermarket."

She said, "Yes, judge."

He said, "What did you steal?"

"A can of peaches," she told him.

Why?"

"I was hungry, Judge."

"How many peaches were in the can?"

"Three."

"Well," the judge said, "I'll have to give you three days in jail."

As soon as he said that, the woman's husband jumped up and said, "Judge, may I say something?"

"Of course."

"She also stole a can of peas."

Well, my wife did not steal from Starbucks, but she took this enclosed book by mistake when we stayed at the Marriott and had coffee at your place. (That's what she says.) She will sleep better tonight knowing that it has been returned; so will I.

SOME SILLY THOUGHTS

A MAN WALKS INTO A PAWN SHOP and asks the owner if he wants to buy a musical instrument. The owner tells him that he might buy it and asks to see the instrument. The man tells him that he is selling his voice, a musical instrument. The owner tells him selling his voice might be a problem. The man answers, "That has been my problem."

———

Many years ago, on a long car trip with my wife and our two children, my younger son, John, and I decided to make up a joke. Here it is.

A proctologist was not very happy doing the work he was doing and had a great desire to find another vocation. He wanted to be a butcher and specialize in preparing the most delicious chickens. He did so and became very famous and rich. The moral of this is: A hand in a bird is worth two in the tush.

———

When Shelly Berman was a child, his mother took him to a

hotel for an overnight stay. When they got on line to register, they were behind a nun. Just as the nun got to the front of the line, Shelly ran before her. Shelly's mother grabbed him and said, "Wait 'til the nun signs, Shelly."

———

An American Indian wanted his son to be educated, so he sent him to a school to learn how to be an electrician. When he graduated with high marks, he came back to his father's home. The father was very proud and asked him to put a light in the outhouse. He became the first person to wire ahead for a reservation.

———

The same Indian made lots of money and decided to buy a boat. He became the first red son in the sail set.

TWO CHARACTERS

D AN AND EUGENE gave you the impression that they were twins, since an identical trait dominated their way of life.

The trait was to be polite to an extreme. Their *excuse me's, thank you's,* and *after you's* were used, in the opinion of many, to a fault.

One day we got together for a musical discussion. Dan and Eugene as polite as ever. When the meeting ended and we were departing, Dan and Eugene waited for everyone to leave first. When they got to the door, Dan said to Eugene, "After you."

Eugene answered, "No after you."

I had already left the room but turned around to see what would happen next. As far as I know, they're still at that door.

HOW TO MAKE
YOUR MARRIAGE BETTER

WHEN I FIRST GOT MARRIED, we had a problem getting to places on time. If we had an appointment for 11:00 a.m. and it would take about half hour to get there, I'd ask my wife to get ready to leave at 10:30. She'd always be about fifteen minutes late. Easy to solve that. Instead of leaving a half hour before the appointment, I have for many years told her that we would be leaving fifteen minutes earlier than necessary. So we're never late.

Also, when we got married and sat down for dinner, I'd ask her what she wanted as a drink—wine, soda, or whatever. When she told me, I'd get up, get a glass, and pour whatever she wanted. She'd tell me I'd poured either too much or not enough. If I did this away from the table, it would mean a couple of trips to get it right. So after a while, I solved the problem. Now, when I'm told what she wants, I bring both the glass and the bottle next to her and start pouring until she tells me when to stop.

I'm less tired after supper now, and she's happier.

These two examples are only two of a hundred I've had to adjust to in my life.

ABOUT MY FRIEND J.P.

W HEN I BECAME music librarian at the Met, one of my very important chores was to have open communication channels with all other opera companies, orchestras, music publishers, related companies, and people connected with the music scene.

In the 1960s, the main means of communication were phone and mail. Since there were many answers to questions, not only I, but other librarians, needed, the phone became our main tool for getting information. As a result, I got to know others mostly by voice.

This all changed in the early 1980s, when a few librarians organized a group called Major Orchestra Librarian's Association (MOLA). We had our first meeting in Philadelphia and still have yearly meetings in different cities all over the States and even in Europe.

At that first gathering in Philadelphia, I got to see many faces that belonged to the voices with whom I had been in touch over the years.

One of the librarians at this first meeting was J.P. (John Perkel). He was a short fellow who reminded me of Woody Allen (he still does), and we became immediate friends.

He had first studied violin and gone to music school, where he realized that the violin was not for him—but he loved music. He got his first job as a librarian with the Buffalo Symphony. Later he worked with the New York Philharmonic and finally with the real love of his life, the Boston Symphony.

Besides his great love of music, his rise to the top of one of the great American orchestras, he had one incredible trait. If he met this person years later, he could recall whatever he had learned at their first meeting: their birthday, whether they were married and had children, their names, and such. He astonished us all. He also could recall most details relating to classical music. Quite a guy! We have remained friends since the 1960s.

What did I say his name was?

THE PIANIST—A FANTASY

CHARLES WOODBURN was born into a very musical family. His father was a violinist in a symphony orchestra, and his sister was a cellist who had recently gotten her first position in another symphony orchestra.

Charles studied piano at a major music school, and after graduating he kept up his private study. He practiced as much as six to eight hours a day. He got to perform in many concerts, but just couldn't make it to the Big Time.

Just before he graduated he had met a lovely young woman, also a student at the music school. They kept up their relationship after graduation. He was not making a living playing the piano, so he decided to get a day job. He was able to get a position in a music store. However, his love of playing the piano never left him. The job at the music store, and the fact that Nancy, his girlfriend, had also gotten a position as a music teacher in a high school, permitted them to get married.

As in most marriages, the first couple of years were fine, but

Charles grew restless. He still wanted to be the concert pianist he dreamed about all the time. They had their first child and hired a nanny, since both of them worked all day.

A short time later, Charles shocked Nancy by telling her he was going to quit his job and try again to become the musician he had such a great drive for. They already had a nanny, and even though their financial life was precarious, he told her that they would have to keep the nanny, so that he could devote all his time to practicing.

The nanny was a special person. She was not a musician and had never studied music but had an incredible sense and feeling for it. As Charles spent most of his days at the piano, the nanny listened and heard something that made her feel that he was just missing a couple of small points to make him a great pianist.

One day, while he was at the piano, and the baby was asleep, and the nanny was in her room with the TV on, he got up to drink a glass of water. As he passed her room, he heard the sound of a piano. He knocked on the door and asked if he could enter. She said, "By all means." What he had heard was the TV on a station showing the movie *The Pianist*. He had heard of it but had never seen it. He sat down. Something about the movie moved him as he had never been moved before. A scene with a German officer particularly affected him.

When the movie ended, the nanny said to him, "The pianist was playing with unbelievable emotion. This is what you need to do."

Charles left the room and did not touch the piano for a couple of days. When he did, he was a different person, and his playing reached new heights. He too, now played with unbelievable emotion.

His brief encounter with the nanny changed his life—and he went on to have a brilliant career.

THERE ARE DAYS

THERE ARE DAYS when I feel lousy, and days when I feel great. Most days, I don't know how I feel.

I wanted to write a song with the title "I'm Feeling Good Today; There's Something Wrong." As silly as this sounds, it's true.

So today, up to now, I'm feeling good.

I'm sure there's something wrong.

THE END

One of the stories I wrote in the Met section of this book describes the concerts I organized, while on tour, for mentally challenged children. As I said there, it was one of the highlights of my life, as it was for everybody who participated.

I started studying music when I was eight years old. I didn't believe I had any talent for composing it. One day, though, I sat down and decided to write a song that would be appropriate for those affairs. I was given a gift, to write one song that everyone told me was perfect. The title is "Good-bye For Now."

Goodbye for now!

Words and music
by John Grande

With Maestro James Levine

With Maestro Nello Santi, 2008

With Joan